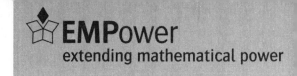

Using Benchmarks

Fractions, Decimals, and Percents

TEACHER BOOK

TERC

Mary Jane Schmitt, Myriam Steinback,
Tricia Donovan, Martha Merson, and Marlene Kliman

Key Curriculum Press
Innovators in Mathematics Education

TERC, Technical Education Research Centers, Inc.
2067 Massachusetts Avenue
Cambridge, Massachusetts 02140

Key College Publishing and Key Curriculum Press:
Development Editor: Erika Shaffer
Production Director: McKinley Williams
Production Project Manager: Ken Wischmeyer
Project Manager: Susan Yates
Consultant: Donna Curry
Text Designer: Laura Murray Productions
Proofreader: Publication Services
Photo Researcher: Laura Murray Productions
Art and Design Coordinator: Jensen Barnes
Cover and Logo Design: Kavitha Becker, Marilyn Perry
Cover Photo Credit: Jensen Barnes
Printer: Alonzo Printing

Editorial Director: Richard J. Bonacci
Vice President/General Manager: Mike Simpson
Publisher: Steven Rasmussen

EMPower Research and Development Team
Principal Investigator: Myriam Steinback
Co-Principal Investigator: Mary Jane Schmitt
Research Associate: Martha Merson
Curriculum Developer: Tricia Donovan

Contributing Authors
Donna Curry
Marlene Kliman

Technical Team
Graphic Designer and Project Assistant: Juania Ashley
Production and Design Coordinator: Valerie Martin
Copyeditor: Jill Pellarin

Evaluation Team
Brett Consulting Group:
Belle Brett
Marilyn Matzko

EMPower™ was developed at TERC in Cambridge, Massachusetts. This material is based upon work supported by the National Science Foundation under award number ESI-9911410. Any opinions, findings, and conclusions or recommendations expressed in this publication are those of the authors and do not necessarily reflect the views of the National Science Foundation.

TERC is a not-for-profit education research and development organization dedicated to improving mathematics, science, and technology teaching and learning.

Key Curriculum Press
1150 65th Street
Emeryville, CA 94608
510-595-7000
editorial@keycollege.com
www.keypress.com

Printed in the United States of America
10 9 8 7 6 5 4 3 2   08 07 06

ISBN 1-55953-729-9

Advisory Board

Donna Curry, Equipped for the Future, National Center
Solange Farina, Math Exchange Group, New York City
Linda Kime, Mathematics Association of America and
    University of Massachusetts, Boston
Ron Kindig, Los Angeles Unified School District (retired)
Kenn Pendleton, General Education Development (GED) Testing Service
Ujwala Samant, National Center for the Study of Adult Learning and Literacy
William Thomas, American Mathematics Association of Two-Year Colleges
    (AMAYTC) and University of Toledo

Consultants and Reviewers

Scott W. Beckett, Jacksonville State University
Sherry Fraser, Interactive Mathematics Program
Arthur G. Fruhling, Yuba Community College
Nancy R. Johnson, Manatee Community College
Steve Monk, University of Washington
Elizabeth Phillips, Connected Mathematics Program
Mark Rudd, Albuquerque TVI
Karen Sitren, Santa Fe Community College
Cornelia Tierney, TERC
Kevin Wheeler, Three Rivers Community College

EMPower Teacher Participants

Arizona

Gila River Indian Community 21st Century
   Community Learning Center, Gila River
Andrea Parrella

Illinois

Adult Education Center, Rock Valley College,
   Rockford
Phyllis Flanagan, Melinda Harrison

Comprehensive Community Solutions, Inc.,
   YouthBuild, Rockford
Ryan Boyce

Township High School District 214
   Community Education, Arlington Heights
Kathy Conrad

Maine

Bailey Evening School, Bath
Pam Bessey

Gardiner Adult and Community Education Program
Diann Bailey

Windham Adult Education, Windham
Eva Giles

Massachusetts

Action for Boston Community Development, Inc.,
   LearningWorks, Boston
Kelly Qualman

Adult Learning Center at Middlesex Community
   College, Bedford
Roberta Froelich

Brockton Adult Learning Center, Brockton
Marilyn Moses

Community Learning Center, Cambridge
Nellie Dedmon, Sylvia Lotspeich Greene,
   Linda Huntington

Dimock Commuity Health Center, Roxbury
Martha Gray

Harvard Bridge to Learning and Literacy, Cambridge
Judy Hikes, Carol Kolenik

Holyoke Adult Learning Opportunities (HALO)
   Center, Holyoke
Kelly Martin, Glenn Yarnell

Hyde Square Task Force, Jamaica Plain
Nora O'Connor

Jewish Vocational Services, Boston
Susan Arase, Terry Lerner, Jeff Snyder

Lowell Adult Education Program, Lowell
Barbara Goodridge

Mount Wachusett Community College, Gardner
Patricia Vorfeld

Notre Dame Education Center, South Boston
Esther D. Leonelli

Pioneer Valley Adult Education Center,
   Northampton
Olu Odusina

Project Place, Boston
Sharon Carey, Maia Hendrickson

Quinsigamond Community College Adult Basic
   Education Program, Worcester
Cathy Coleman

Read/Write/Now, Springfield
Lee E. Boone, Susanne Campagna, Michelle Faith
   Brown, Lucille Fandel

Somerville Center for Adult Learning Experiences
   (SCALE), Somerville
Tom Glannon

X-Cel Adult Education, Dorchester
Don Sands

New Jersey

New Brunswick Public Schools—Adult Learning Center, New Brunswick
Jacqueline Arkoe, Phyllis Boulanger, Sue Helfand, Karen C. Pickering

New York

Adult Learning Center, La Guardia Community College, Long Island City
Norma Andrade, Mark Trushkowsky

BEGIN Managed Programs, New York
Charles Brover, Solange Farina, Santiago Perez, Elizabeth Reddin

Borough of Manhattan Community College/CUNY Adult Basic Education Program, Center for Continuing Education and Workforce Development, New York
Elliot Fink, Mark Lance

City University of New York, Continuing Education, New York
Lisa Simon

Lehman Adult Learning Center, Bronx
Deidre Freeman

SafeSpace-LifeSkills, New York
Jonna Rao

The Adult Learning Center, College of Staten Island, Staten Island
Karen Johnsen

Pennsylvania

Lancaster-Lebanon Intermediate Unit 13/Career Link, Lancaster
Margaret Giordano, Barbara Tyndall

Rhode Island

Dorcas Place, Parent Literacy Center, Providence
Shannon Dolan, Jerelyn Thomas

Tennessee

Hawkins County Adult Education Program, Rogersville
Lisa Mullins

Acknowledgments

Many friends and family members supported the teachers' and EMPower's efforts. Thank you, Denise Deagan, Judith Diamond, Cara Dimattia, Ellen McDevitt, Sandy Strunk, and the board of the Adult Numeracy Network. Roberta Froelich, Brad Hamilton, Michael Hanish, David Hayes, Judy Hikes, Alisa Izumi, Esther D. Leonelli, Myra Love, Lambrina Mileva, Luz Rivas, Johanna Schmitt, Rachael Stark, Jonathan Steinback, and Sean Sutherland all made unique and timely contributions to the project.

We appreciate the encouragement and advice from John (Spud) Bradley, EMPower's program officer, and Gerhard Salinger of the National Science Foundation.

We are indebted to every adult student who participated in the piloting of EMPower. Their honest feedback and suggestions for what worked and what did not work were invaluable. We could not have completed the curriculum without them or their teachers.

Contents

Introduction to the EMPower Curriculum

Background

Extending Mathematical Power (EMPower) integrates recent mathematics education reform into the field of education for adults and out-of-school youth. EMPower was designed especially for those students who return for a second chance at education by enrolling in remedial and adult basic education programs, high school equivalency programs, and developmental programs at community colleges. However, the curriculum is appropriate for a variety of other settings as well, such as high schools, workplaces, and parent and paraprofessional education programs. EMPower builds interest and competency in mathematical problem solving and communication.

Over the course of four years (2000–2004), a collaboration of teachers and researchers with expertise in adult numeracy education and K–12 mathematics reform developed and piloted eight contextualized curriculum units. These units are organized around four central topics: number and operation sense; patterns, functions, and relations; geometry and measurement; and data and graphs. The EMPower program serves as a model for a cohesive mathematics curriculum that offers content consistent with the *Principles and Standards for School Mathematics* (NCTM, 2000), as well as frameworks that are adult-focused, such as the *Equipped for the Future Content Standards* (Stein, 2000), the *Massachusetts ABE Curriculum Frameworks for Mathematics and Numeracy* (Massachusetts Department of Education, 2001), and the Adult Numeracy Network's *Framework for Adult Numeracy Standards* (Curry, Schmitt, & Waldron, 1996). The curriculum fosters a pedagogy of learning for understanding; it embeds teacher support and is transformative, yet realistic, for multi-level classrooms.

EMPower challenges students and teachers to consistently extend their ideas of what it means to do math. The curriculum focuses on mathematical reasoning, communication, and problem solving with a variety of approaches and strategies, not just rote memorization and symbol manipulation. The program fosters a learning community in which students are encouraged to expand their understanding of mathematics through open-ended investigations, working collaboratively, sharing ideas, and discovering multiple ways for solving problems. The goal of EMPower is to help people build experience managing the mathematical demands of various life situations, such as finances and commerce, interpretation of news stories, and leisure activities, and to connect those experiences to mathematical principles.

A Focus on Mathematical Content

The EMPower curriculum supports students' and teachers' growth by directing attention to significant mathematical understandings.

EMPower emphasizes:

- Data analysis, geometry and measurement, algebra, and numbers and operations at all student levels.

- Reliance on benchmark numbers—such as powers and multiples of 10, common fractions, and their decimal and percent equivalents—for making mental calculations.

- Early use of calculators to support computation.

- Development of reasoning on proportion and parts of quantities before consideration of formal operations with rational numbers.

- Making decisions about data where students generate, as well as interpret, graphical representations.

- Geometry and measurement based on opportunities to see and touch in developing an understanding of spatial relationships and formulas.

- Leading with patterns and relationships in contextual situations and the representations of these situations with diagrams, tables, graphs, verbal rules, and symbolic notation to develop algebraic competence.

A Focus on Pedagogy

Mathematics is meaningful within a social context. While mathematical truths are universal, the meaning and relevance of numbers changes according to the setting and culture. Therefore, the EMPower pedagogy is focused on sets of connected activities that require communication and discourse.

EMPower asks students to

- Work collaboratively with others on open-ended investigations;

- Share strategies orally and in writing; and

- Justify answers in multiple ways.

Key features of curriculum activities provide

- Clear mathematical goals;

- Contexts that are engaging and useful for young people and adults;

- Opportunities to strengthen mathematical language and communication skills;

- Various ways of entering and solving problems; and

- Puzzles that draw students into problems and motivate them to seek a solution.

Overview of EMPower Units
Features of the Teacher Book

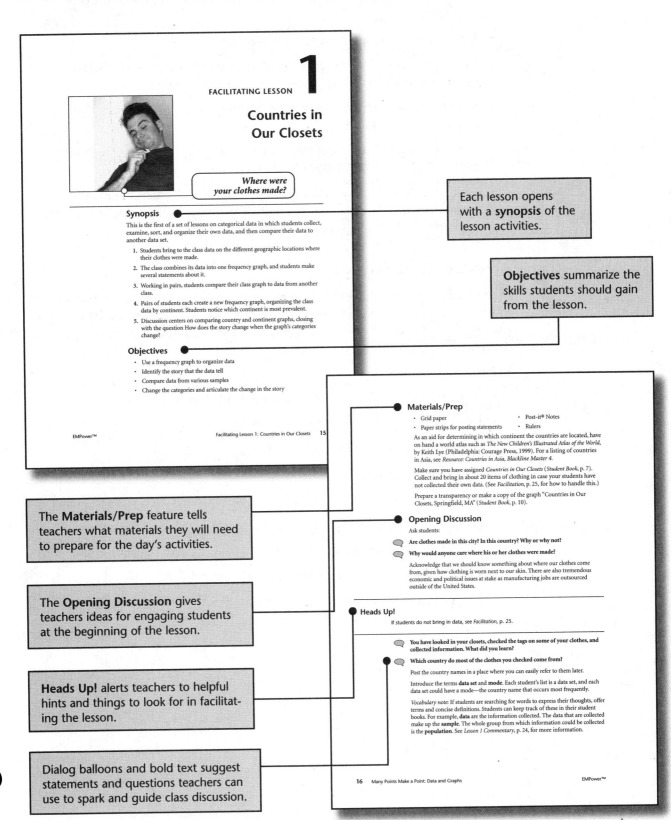

FACILITATING LESSON 1

Countries in Our Closets

Where were your clothes made?

Synopsis

This is the first of a set of lessons on categorical data in which students collect, examine, sort, and organize their own data, and then compare their data to another data set.

1. Students bring to the class data on the different geographic locations where their clothes were made.
2. The class combines its data into one frequency graph, and students make several statements about it.
3. Working in pairs, students compare their class graph to data from another class.
4. Pairs of students each create a new frequency graph, organizing the class data by continent. Students notice which continent is most prevalent.
5. Discussion centers on comparing country and continent graphs, closing with the question How does the story change when the graph's categories change?

Objectives

- Use a frequency graph to organize data
- Identify the story that the data tell
- Compare data from various samples
- Change the categories and articulate the change in the story

Each lesson opens with a **synopsis** of the lesson activities.

Objectives summarize the skills students should gain from the lesson.

Materials/Prep

- Grid paper
- Paper strips for posting statements
- Post-it® Notes
- Rulers

As an aid for determining in which continent the countries are located, have on hand a world atlas such as *The New Children's Illustrated Atlas of the World*, by Keith Lye (Philadelphia: Courage Press, 1999). For a listing of countries in Asia, see *Resource: Countries in Asia, Blackline Master 4*.

Make sure you have assigned *Countries in Our Closets* (*Student Book*, p. 7). Collect and bring in about 20 items of clothing in case your students have not collected their own data. (See *Facilitation*, p. 25, for how to handle this.)

Prepare a transparency or make a copy of the graph "Countries in Our Closets, Springfield, MA" (*Student Book*, p. 10).

Opening Discussion

Ask students:

💬 **Are clothes made in this city? In this country? Why or why not?**

💬 **Why would anyone care where his or her clothes were made?**

Acknowledge that we should know something about where our clothes come from, given how clothing is worn next to our skin. There are also tremendous economic and political issues at stake as manufacturing jobs are outsourced outside of the United States.

Heads Up!

If students do not bring in data, see *Facilitation*, p. 25.

💬 **You have looked in your closets, checked the tags on some of your clothes, and collected information. What did you learn?**

💬 **Which country do most of the clothes you checked come from?**

Post the country names in a place where you can easily refer to them later.

Introduce the terms **data set** and **mode**. Each student's list is a data set, and each data set could have a mode—the country name that occurs most frequently.

Vocabulary note: If students are searching for words to express their thoughts, offer terms and concise definitions. Students can keep track of these in their student books. For example, **data** are the information collected. The data that are collected make up the **sample**. The whole group from which information could be collected is the **population**. See *Lesson 1 Commentary*, p. 24, for more information.

The **Materials/Prep** feature tells teachers what materials they will need to prepare for the day's activities.

The **Opening Discussion** gives teachers ideas for engaging students at the beginning of the lesson.

Heads Up! alerts teachers to helpful hints and things to look for in facilitating the lesson.

Dialog balloons and bold text suggest statements and questions teachers can use to spark and guide class discussion.

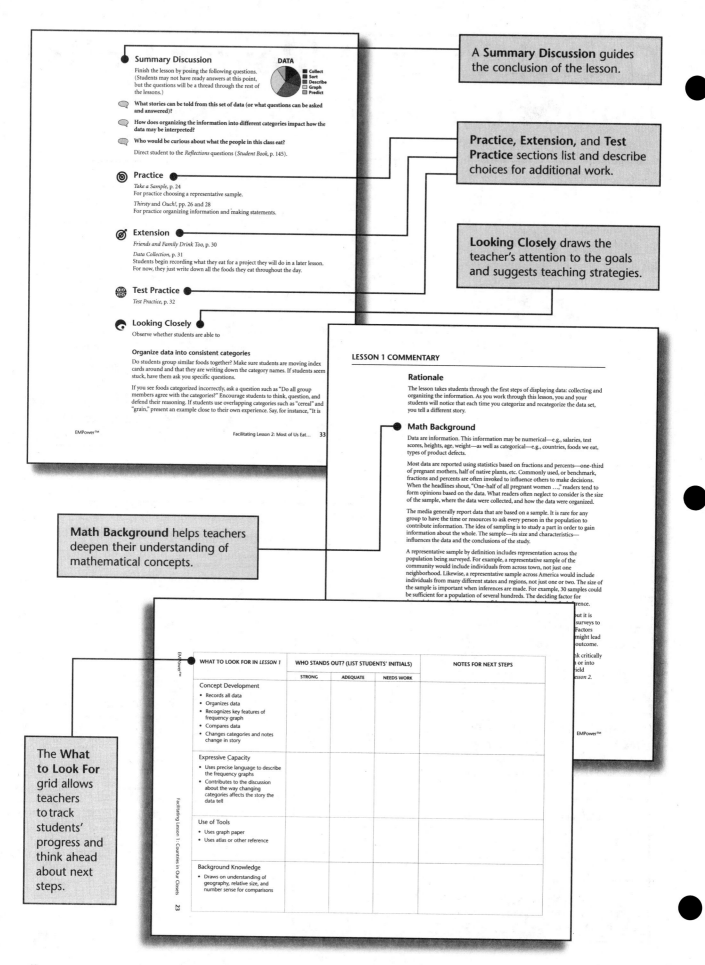

Summary Discussion

Finish the lesson by posing the following questions. (Students may not have ready answers at this point, but the questions will be a thread through the rest of the lessons.)

DATA
- Collect
- Sort
- Describe
- Graph
- Predict

What stories can be told from this set of data (or what questions can be asked and answered)?

How does organizing the information into different categories impact how the data may be interpreted?

Who would be curious about what the people in this class eat?

Direct student to the *Reflections* questions (*Student Book*, p. 145).

Practice

Take a Sample, p. 24
For practice choosing a representative sample.

Thirsty and *Ouch!*, pp. 26 and 28
For practice organizing information and making statements.

Extension

Friends and Family Drink Too, p. 30

Data Collection, p. 31
Students begin recording what they eat for a project they will do in a later lesson. For now, they just write down all the foods they eat throughout the day.

Test Practice

Test Practice, p. 32

Looking Closely

Observe whether students are able to

Organize data into consistent categories
Do students group similar foods together? Make sure students are moving index cards around and that they are writing down the category names. If students seem stuck, have them ask you specific questions.

If you see foods categorized incorrectly, ask a question such as "Do all group members agree with the categories?" Encourage students to think, question, and defend their reasoning. If students use overlapping categories such as "cereal" and "grain," present an example close to their own experience. Say, for instance, "It is

---

LESSON 1 COMMENTARY

Rationale

The lesson takes students through the first steps of displaying data: collecting and organizing the information. As you work through this lesson, you and your students will notice that each time you categorize and recategorize the data set, you tell a different story.

Math Background

Data are information. This information may be numerical—e.g., salaries, test scores, heights, age, weight—as well as categorical—e.g., countries, foods we eat, types of product defects.

Most data are reported using statistics based on fractions and percents—one-third of pregnant mothers, half of native plants, etc. Commonly used, or benchmark, fractions and percents are often invoked to influence others to make decisions. When the headlines shout, "One-half of all pregnant women …," readers tend to form opinions based on the data. What readers often neglect to consider is the size of the sample, where the data were collected, and how the data were organized.

The media generally report data that are based on a sample. It is rare for any group to have the time or resources to ask every person in the population to contribute information. The idea of sampling is to study a part in order to gain information about the whole. The sample—its size and characteristics—influences the data and the conclusions of the study.

A representative sample by definition includes representation across the population being surveyed. For example, a representative sample of the community would include individuals from across town, not just one neighborhood. Likewise, a representative sample across America would include individuals from many different states and regions, not just one or two. The size of the sample is important when inferences are made. For example, 30 samples could be sufficient for a population of several hundreds. The deciding factor for

…ut it is …surveys to …Factors …might lead …outcome.

…nk critically …n or into …field …esson 2.

EMPower™

WHAT TO LOOK FOR IN *LESSON 1*	WHO STANDS OUT? (LIST STUDENTS' INITIALS)			NOTES FOR NEXT STEPS
	STRONG	ADEQUATE	NEEDS WORK	
Concept Development • Records all data • Organizes data • Recognizes key features of frequency graph • Compares data • Changes categories and notes change in story				
Expressive Capacity • Uses precise language to describe the frequency graphs • Contributes to the discussion about the way changing categories affects the story the data tell				
Use of Tools • Uses graph paper • Uses atlas or other reference				
Background Knowledge • Draws on understanding of geography, relative size, and number sense for comparisons				

A Summary Discussion guides the conclusion of the lesson.

Practice, Extension, and **Test Practice** sections list and describe choices for additional work.

Looking Closely draws the teacher's attention to the goals and suggests teaching strategies.

Math Background helps teachers deepen their understanding of mathematical concepts.

The **What to Look For** grid allows teachers to track students' progress and think ahead about next steps.

The authors give ideas for **Making the Lesson Easier** and **Making the Lesson Harder**.

Context

Some students may know about *maquiladoras* in Mexican border towns, where women make clothes for very little money and with no benefits or environmental Occupational Safety and Health Administration (OSHA) workplace protections. CorpWatch (www.corpwatch.org) is one source for information on *maquiladoras*.

Facilitation

If students do not bring in data, or if their sample is too small, skip the second part of the *Opening Discussion*. Have available a pile of 20 clothing articles with labels. First, ask students to predict where the clothes were made. Post the list of their guesses. Note that it will be hard for them to answer this question unless they organize the information on the labels. Then divide up the 20 articles of clothing. Have students write the name of the country for each piece of clothing on a Post-it Note, one country name per note. Ask: "Where are most of our clothes made?" Then continue with the activity.

Making the Lesson Easier

Frequency graphs lend themselves to comparisons among categories. If students have little fluency stating comparisons, you may choose only to compare size, using terms like "greater," "fewest," or "less than." For students who are encountering data formally for the first time, the notion that collapsing data yields different stories may be difficult. Treat this lightly in the activity, and revisit such questions after students have more experience categorizing and recategorizing data in the homework and in *Lesson 2*.

Making the Lesson Harder

If your students can handle benchmark fractions and percents, get them to look critically at the data, including the source and sample size. You might ask:

💬 If we asked another class what countries are in their closets, what do you think would happen to the categories? What if we asked the entire community?

💬 How do you think your data would compare to data from another class of adult students in another community?

If students struggle with the idea of sample, you might try this: Have them each write their favorite color on a Post-it Note. If you have a small class, ask them to write the color on two Post-it Notes. Place all of the notes in a container. Have someone randomly (eyes closed) choose a few notes from the container and place them across a line to form a frequency graph. Ask the students how they think this sample compares to the actual total number of colors on notes in the container. You can have them do another frequency graph to compare the sample to the actual total.

LESSON 1 IN ACTION

Alice articulates the mathematical principle behind compressed data.

> I asked, "How did the change in categories affect what we noticed about the data?"
>
> Alice answered, "Well, we keep losing information."
>
> "How so?"
>
> Patiently, Alice explained that when we started our work, every bit of data was visible. She added that we had lost details initially recorded. "At first, we knew every country in every person's closet and how many pieces of clothing came from that country. Then we combined the data, and we lost track of who had which countries. Then we did it by continent, and we lost track of all the countries."
>
> Alice's realization quickly gained agreement from the rest of the class. After all, just the previous week a classmate had noted, "When you change the amount of data you look at, you find different things."
>
> Sonia added her comment with increased conviction: "It is like politics. Politicians use a graph and tell you this is true, but you look at the graph, and it does not tell you everything."
>
> *Tricia Donovan*
> *Pioneer Valley Adult Education Center, Northampton, MA*

In **Lesson in Action**, EMPower teachers share their classroom experiences.

Overview of EMPower Units
Features of the Student Book

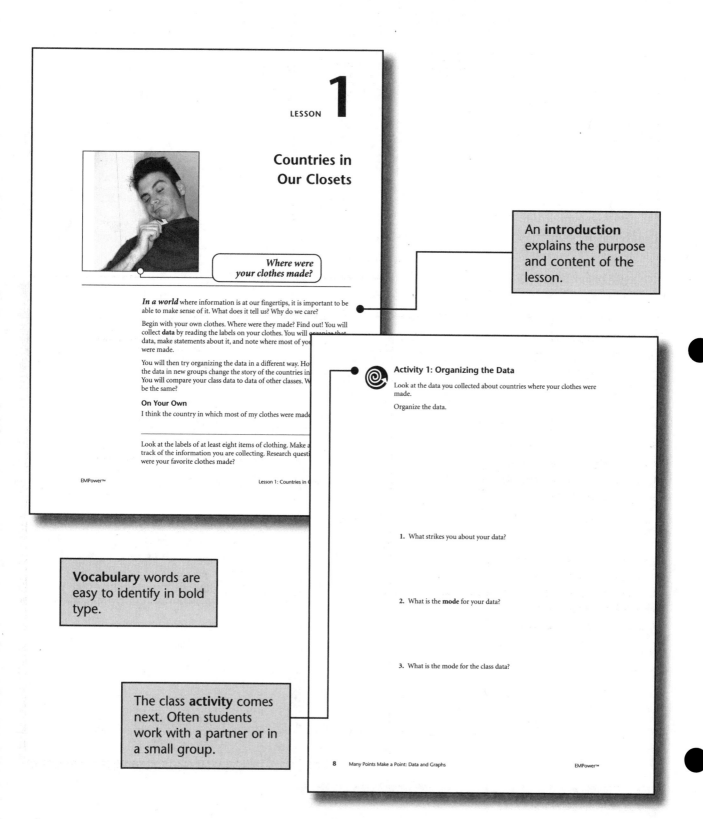

LESSON **1**

Countries in Our Closets

Where were your clothes made?

An **introduction** explains the purpose and content of the lesson.

In a world where information is at our fingertips, it is important to be able to make sense of it. What does it tell us? Why do we care?

Begin with your own clothes. Where were they made? Find out! You will collect **data** by reading the labels on your clothes. You will organize that data, make statements about it, and note where most of you~~r clothes~~ were made.

You will then try organizing the data in a different way. Ho~~w~~ the data in new groups change the story of the countries in You will compare your class data to data of other classes. W be the same?

On Your Own

I think the country in which most of my clothes were made

Look at the labels of at least eight items of clothing. Make a track of the information you are collecting. Research questi~~on~~ were your favorite clothes made?

EMPower™   Lesson 1: Countries in

Vocabulary words are easy to identify in bold type.

Activity 1: Organizing the Data

Look at the data you collected about countries where your clothes were made.

Organize the data.

1. What strikes you about your data?

2. What is the **mode** for your data?

3. What is the mode for the class data?

The class **activity** comes next. Often students work with a partner or in a small group.

8   Many Points Make a Point: Data and Graphs   EMPower™

Practice: Categorically Speaking

Sometimes we can organize categories into subgroups of other categories in order to better understand the data. For example, drug stores will often organize their aisles by category—skin care, beauty aids, and so on. Then the items in each of those aisles are also organized. This makes it easier to take inventory and place orders and for the customer to find products.

Can you think of other examples where information is categorized?

Use the chart below *or* create your own chart; draw a picture; make a list; or write about examples you see at home or at work. In the chart below, one example is given.

Location	What Stuff or Information?	How Is It Organized?
Drug store	Over-the-counter products they sell	Skin care Stationery Beauty aids First aid Seasonal Hair care

Extension: Taking Inventory

Find a drawer or closet filled with many things. Use a frequency graph to show the contents. Start with six categories. Then do another frequency graph to show the same items, but this time use three categories.

For example:

My Medicine Cabinet

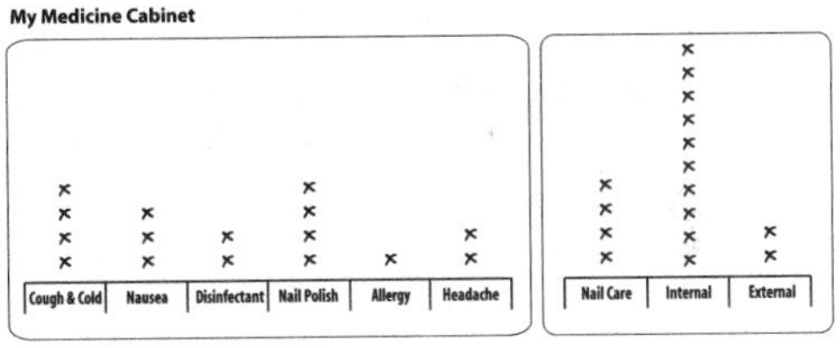

Test Practice

> A **Test Practice** that reflects the format of the GED test concludes each lesson.

1. Freda worked at a printing press. She kept a tally of all the defects she found in the books she was processing. Based on the frequency graph she created, shownbelow, which of the following statements is true?

(1) There were more defects related to colors than any other defect.

(2) There were twice as many torn pages as there were warped spines.

(3) There were more warped spines than colors that bled.

(4) Half of all the defects were related to colors that bled.

(5) Half of all the defects were related to pages that were torn.

Book Defects Frequency Graph

| Pages Torn | Colors Bled | Uncut Pages | Spine Warped | Faded Colors |

2. Tony, a tour guide, has been keeping a tally of visitors from different states. According to his tally, which of the following is *not* a true statement?

(1) The fewest number of visitors came from Oregon.

(2) There were as many visitors from Maine as there were from Georgia.

(3) There were as many visitors from Georgia as there were from Oregon and Texas.

(4) There were twice as many visitors from Florida as there were from Rhode Island.

(5) There were twice as many visitors from Idaho as there were from Maine.

U.S. Tourist Frequency Graph

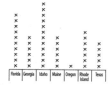

| Florida | Georgia | Idaho | Maine | Oregon | Rhode Island | Texas |

3. Clara is paid a commission on each of the large electronics devices that she sells. She tallied the different items she sold for the month. Based on her tally, what can she tell her boss about her sales?

(1) She sold twice as many DVD players as she did TVs.

(2) She sold twice as many DVD players as she did computers.

(3) She sold more DVD players than she did TVs and computers combined.

(4) She sold more TVs and VCRs than she did stereos and DVD players combined.

(5) She sold half as many TVs as she did stereos.

Home Media Frequency Graph

4. Bronson, a forest ranger in the Green Mountains, kept track of the different animals that were reportedly seen in one of the campgrounds during the month of May. Based on his tally, which of the following statements could he tell the media?

(1) There were twice as many wolves reportedly seen as bears.

(2) Half of all the reported sightings were wolves.

(3) There were more bears than wolves reportedly seen.

(4) There were twice as many moose reportedly seen than there were black bears.

(5) One-quarter of all reported sightings were brown bears.

North American Wildlife Frequency Graph

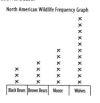

| Black Bears | Brown Bears | Moose | Wolves |

5. According to Global Exchange, some workers in China who make clothing for Disney are paid as little as $0.16 per hour. At this wage, what amount would a worker make for a 40-hour workweek?

(1) $64.00

(2) $6.40

(3) $6.00

(4) $80.00

(5) $0.60

6. In 2003 the U.S. Department of Labor (DOL) issued new regulations for overtime pay. The DOL estimated that under the new regulations 1.3 million low-wage workers would become eligible for overtime pay, unless their wages were raised to $425 per week. The DOL estimated that 24.8 percent of those workers were Hispanic and 16.6 percent were African American. What percent were neither Hispanic nor African American?

Changing the Culture

The authors have created this curriculum to follow the National Council of Teachers of Mathematics (NCTM) Principles and Standards; however, teachers who use EMPower face the challenge of transforming the prevailing culture of their math classrooms. EMPower pilot teachers offer some ideas for facilitating this transition:

■ Set the stage. As a class, set ground rules. Explicitly state that this is a space for everyone to learn. As one teacher said, "We are in this together. Share, even if you do not think you are right. Whatever you add will be helpful. It lets us see how you are looking at things."

■ Group your students. Match students whose learning styles and background knowledge complement each other. Ask questions, such as How did it go to work together? How did everyone contribute?

■ Allow wait time. Studies have shown that teachers often wait less than three seconds before asking another question. Students need more time to think.

■ Sit down. Watch students before interrupting to help them. Listen for logic and evidence of understanding. Follow the thread of students' thinking to uncover unconventional approaches. During discussions with the whole group, hand over the chalk.

■ Review written work. Look beyond right and wrong answers to learn everything you can about what a student knows. Determine what seems solid and easy, as well as patterns in errors. If students are scattered, suggest ways they can organize their work; this is likely to lead to more efficient problem solving and clearer communication.

■ Question. Hearing the right answer is not necessarily a cue to move on. Question students at this point too. Specific questions are included in the lesson facilitation.

Unit Sequences and Connections

The sequence in which the EMPower units can be used effectively with your class will depend on the backgrounds and interests of students. The units are not numbered, so teachers can order them according to their class needs; however, the authors suggest specific unit arrangements that will support students' progression through certain concepts.

The authors do not recommend sequencing the units according to the traditional basic math model that begins with whole numbers and follows with fractions, decimals, and percents; data and graphs; algebra; and then geometry. Instead, they suggest you integrate the five units that focus on numbers with the units on geometry, data, and algebra. The authors found that this integration of topics helped to motivate the adult students in their pilot classes.

Although the units were not specifically designed to build on one another, there are clear connections between some of the units in the series. *Over, Around, and Within: Geometry and Measurement* provides a nice introduction to the program because it focuses on small whole numbers. *Everyday Number Sense: Mental Math and Visual Models* could follow to further develop whole number mental math skills and visual models. *Using Benchmarks: Fractions, Decimals, and Percents* provides the necessary groundwork with fractions, decimals, and percents to describe approximate relationships between data sets in *Many Points Make a Point: Data and Graphs*. And

Split It Up: More Fractions, Decimals, and Percents continues to expand students' repertoire of familiar fractions, decimals, and percents. *Seeking Patterns, Building Rules: Algebraic Thinking* builds upon the tools and relationships used in *Keeping Things in Proportion: Reasoning with Ratios*; finally, *Operations Sense: Even More Fractions, Decimals, and Percents* introduces more complex fractions and operations in geometric, graphic, and algebraic contexts. The following diagram demonstrates this integrated sequence:

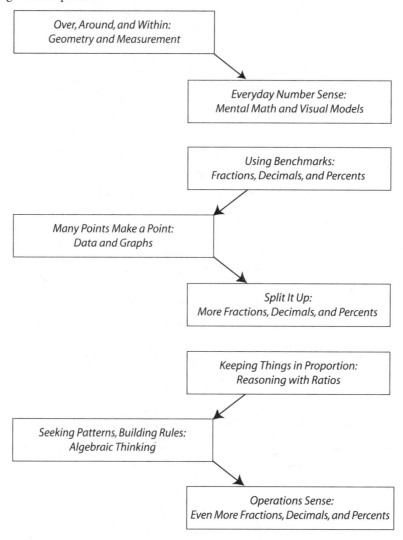

Unit Descriptions

Over, Around, and Within: Geometry and Measurement
Students explore the features and measures of basic shapes. Perimeter and area of two-dimensional shapes and volume of rectangular solids provide the focus.

Everyday Number Sense: Mental Math and Visual Models
Students solve problems and compute with whole numbers using mental math strategies with benchmarks of 1, 10, 100, and 1,000. Number lines, arrays, and diagrams support their conceptual understanding of number relationships and the four operations.

Using Benchmarks: Fractions, Decimals, and Percents
Students use the fractions ½, ¼, ¾, and ¹⁄₁₀; the decimals 0.1, 0.5, 0.25, and 0.75; and the percents 50%, 25%, 75%, 100%, and the multiples of 10% as benchmarks to describe and compare all part-whole relationships.

Many Points Make a Point: Data and Graphs
Students collect, organize, and represent data using frequency, bar, and circle graphs. They use line graphs to describe change over time. They use benchmark fractions and the three measures of central tendency—mode, median, and mean—to describe sets of data.

Split It Up: More Fractions, Decimals, and Percents
Building on their command of common benchmark fractions, students add thirds, eighths, and hundredths and their decimal and percent equivalents to their repertoire of part-whole relationships.

Keeping Things in Proportion: Reasoning with Ratios
Students use various tools—objects, diagrams, tables, graphs, and equations—to understand proportional and nonproportional relationships.

Seeking Patterns, Building Rules: Algebraic Thinking
Students use a variety of representational tools—diagrams, words, tables, graphs, and equations—to understand linear patterns and functions. They connect the rate of change with the slope of a line and compare linear with nonlinear relationships. They also gain facility with and comprehension of basic algebraic notation.

Operation Sense: Even More Fractions, Decimals, and Percents
Students extend their understanding of the four operations with whole numbers as they puzzle over questions such as "How is it possible that two fractions multiplied might yield a smaller amount than either fraction?" and "What does it mean to divide one-half by six?"

Frequently Asked Questions

Q: I have classes that are widely multi-level. Can this work?

A: Many teachers see a wide range of levels within the group as an obstacle. Turn the range of levels to your advantage. Focus on students' representations (words, graphs, equations, sketches). This gives everyone the chance to see that answers emerge in several ways. Slowing down deepens understanding and avoids facile responses. Having calculators available can even the playing field. Implement the suggestions in *Making the Lesson Easier* and *Making the Lesson Harder* of each lesson facilitation in the *Lesson Commentary* sections.

Q: How do I deal with erratic attendance patterns?

A: Uneven attendance can be disruptive. Students who miss class may feel disoriented; however, the lessons spiral back to the most important concepts. When the curriculum circles back, students will have a chance to revisit concepts and get a toehold.

Q: What do I do if I run out of time, and there is no way to finish a lesson?

A: Each activity is important, but reviewing it is equally important. It is better to cut the activity short so there is time to talk with students about what they noticed. Maximize the time by selecting a student or group whose work you feel will add to the class's understanding to report their findings. Be conscious of when you are letting an activity go on too long because the energy is high. Fun is good, but be sure important learning is happening. If you like to give time in class to reviewing homework, and you want to hear from everyone in discussions, you will run out of time. Schedule a catch-up session every three or four lessons.

Q: *How do I respond to comments such as "Can't we go back to the old way?"*

A: Change is unsettling, especially for students who are accustomed to math classes where their job is to work silently on a worksheet solving problems by following a straightforward example. Be clear about the reasons why you have chosen to de-emphasize some of the traditional ways of teaching in favor of this approach. Ultimately, you may need to agree to some changes to accommodate students' input. Meanwhile, stick with the curriculum. Reiterate for students what they have accomplished. When there is an "Aha!" moment, point it out.

Q: *My own math background is not strong. Will I be able to teach this curriculum?*

A: Yes! Most teachers tend to teach the way they were taught. Adopting a different stance requires support, and the more types of support, the better. This curriculum offers support in a few ways. The teacher book for each unit lists open-ended questions designed to keep the math on track. In the *Lesson Commentary* sections, the *Math Background* helps teachers deepen their understanding of a concept. In addition, the *Lesson in Action* sections provide examples of student work with comments that illuminate the underlying mathematics.

The best support often comes from a colleague. If no one at your site is currently teaching EMPower, join the Adult Numeracy Network, http://shell04.theworld.com/ std/anpn, and attend your regional NCTM conference. Look for others who are integrating the NCTM Principles and Standards through the use of a curriculum such as *The Investigations in Number, Data, and Space Curriculum* (Russell, S. J., et al., 1998); *Connected Mathematics* (Lappan et al., 1998); or *Interactive Mathematics Program* (Fendel et al., 1997).

Unit Introduction
Using Benchmarks: Fractions, Decimals, and Percents

Where and when are adults most likely to use fractions, decimals, and percents? This question guided the development of EMPower's beginning unit on rational numbers, *Using Benchmarks: Fractions, Decimals, and Percents*. Our observation is that in everyday life, people often use fractions as a way to express the relationship between a part and a whole to answer questions such as: What portion of the population voted in the last election? What part of my paycheck goes to taxes? Are we more than half way there? What part of the day do I spend working?

A second observation is that adults are likely to see fractions and percents as signals to determine a partial amount of a total amount when asking such questions as: How much will I save on the coat that is marked 25% off? What is a 15% tip on this restaurant bill? If I put aside 1/10 of my paycheck each week for "fun money," what will that mean?

And finally, whether comparing a part with its whole or finding a portion of the whole, numerate adults tend to think and speak in familiar numbers, which we refer to as "benchmarks." These ideas led to the selection of the unit's three major themes.

Major Themes

Using friendly fractions, decimals, and percents as benchmarks

> *Encouraging students to consider. . . benchmarks or referents is a way of helping them develop better conceptual understanding of fractions, decimals, and percentages. This intuitive understanding is a priority and should precede the study of operating with fractions, decimals, and percentages* (Developing Number Sense in the Middle Grades, The Addenda Series, Grades 5-8, *1991, p. 10).*

Although this statement was written about developing number sense in school-age children, it makes sense for adults as well. In the real world, numerate adults gravitate to friendly numbers: $7.99 is about eight dollars; 2.254 is a little more than 2 1/4; 1,744,542 is nearly 1 3/4 million. We call such friendly numbers "benchmarks" because they serve as points of reference by which to judge less familiar numbers. Benchmarks not only allow us to arrive at reasonable estimates, they also ground work with other fractions, decimals, and percents.

In this unit, lessons begin with the familiar fraction 1/2 and build on what people know intuitively about Halving. Students start by showing half and move on to discuss how they know it is one-half. Once they establish that a part is half of the whole (by dividing the whole by two or by separating items into two groups), they use this knowledge to determine whether other fractions are larger or smaller than 1/2. Students then move on to the benchmark 1/4. Again, they start by showing what they know. They then consider the fraction 3/4 and how fractions compare with all the benchmark fractions before considering 0.1 and 10%, both equivalent to 1/10.

Understanding a fraction as the relationship between a part and a whole

Students are first asked to focus on fractions as the relationship between two quantities, a part and a whole. They visualize part-whole relationships in a variety of ways—by drawing pictures and using number line segments, area models, sets of discrete objects, and arrays to increase their repertoires.

Understanding a fraction as a part-whole relationship also requires an understanding of the whole as the sum of its parts. To that end, the unit includes activities and practices that focus on the need for fraction complements, such as 1/2 and 1/2, 1/4 and 3/4, or 1/10 and 9/10, to always equal the whole.

Understanding a fraction as a signal to find a portion of something

"I keep only 3/4 of my monthly earnings of $800." "I heard the budget for education might be slashed by a quarter. What does that mean in dollars?" Helping adults address these useful applications of fractions, decimals, and percents is essential.

Students are asked to solve problems in which they find portions of amounts by exploring everyday situations. As part of this exploration, students not only find the fractional part when they know the whole but also, given the fractional part, are asked to find the whole. The lessons go further than simply mirroring the problems adults see in their daily lives. The activities presented in the lessons work to surface methods for visualizing and explaining rational numbers that result in students moving beyond memorization of rules.

Why Are Fractions Harder to Understand than Whole Numbers?

Learning about rational numbers is more complicated and difficult than learning about whole numbers. Rational numbers are more complex than whole numbers, in part because they are represented in several ways . . . and used in many ways . . . (Adding It Up, 2001, p. 231).

This comment makes sense. Every rational number has multiple representations, and every rational number has several meanings. This complexity should not be underestimated.

Each rational number has an infinite number of equivalent representations: 3/4 = 6/8 = 9/12, and so on; 0.75 = 0.750 = 0.7500, and so on; and 75% = 75.0% = 75.00%, and so on. In this unit, students are asked early on to make sense of these equivalencies.

The many meanings of a rational number present another challenge. Again, consider the simple fraction 3/4. The *part-whole relationship* and the fraction as a signal to find a particular *portion of an amount* are not the only meanings of that fraction. Three-fourths can indicate the *division* of 3 by 4 (3 ÷ 4). The fraction 3/4 can also be seen as the relative relationship between any two quantities, not necessarily a part-whole relationship, such as the *ratio* of 3 parts sugar to 4 parts flour in a baking mixture. Finally, 3/4 can name a *position on a number line* that is between 1/2 and 1. Given these five meanings of that one representation, it is no wonder that adults as well as children find fractions confusing!

Proficiency with rational numbers requires a rich and integrated understanding of their various forms and meanings. This mathematical proficiency depends upon opportunities to explore each of these forms and meanings in sufficient depth.

EMPower's approach to fractions, decimals, and percents offers many such opportunities for students to build depth for all five meanings of a fraction. The part-whole model and the portion of an amount model for fractions is central to both *Using Benchmarks: Fractions, Decimals, and Percents* (this unit) and *Split It Up: More Fractions, Decimals, and Percents*. Other models for fractions surface elsewhere in the EMPower series. In *Seeking Patterns, Building Rules: Algebraic Thinking*, students encounter the fraction representing a division relationship ($a/b = a \div b$). In *Keeping Things in Proportion: Reasoning with Ratios*, students grapple with the concept of fractions representing comparative relationships where $a/b = a{:}b$ and with the question "How many a's are there for every number of b's?" In *Operations: Even More Fractions, Decimals, and Percents*, rational numbers are further considered as objects on the number line with which to perform the four operations: addition, subtraction, multiplication, and division.

Unit Goals

By the end of this unit, students should be able to

- Describe part-whole situations in terms of fractions;

- Use objects, diagrams, number line segments, and arrays to represent part-whole situations;

- Determine whether a wide variety of fractions are more than, less than, or equal to the benchmark fractions 1/2, 1/4, 3/4, and 1/10;

- Read benchmark decimals such as 0.1 as fractions;

- Connect percent names with benchmark fractions and decimals.

The Flow of the Unit

There are six lessons with embedded ongoing assessments as well as two separate assessments in the opening and closing sessions (see *Assessments*, pp. xxiv-xxv, for more detail). During the first four lessons, the emphasis is on benchmark fractions (1/2, 1/4, and 3/4) and comparing portions of two- and three-digit whole numbers using those benchmarks. In *Lessons 5* and *6*, the emphasis shifts to decimals, in particular, tenths.

Each lesson has one or more activities or investigations. Allowing time for opening and summary discussions (including time for students to write reflections) and assuming a thoughtful pace, most lessons will exceed an hour. Students' reading and writing levels will have an effect on how long each lesson takes.

In *Lesson 1*, students consider the fraction 1/2 and

- Identify the part and the whole in various cases;

- Consider whether a fractional amount is more than, less than, or equal to 1/2;

- State the fraction that represents the whole for any case.

In *Lesson 2*, students

- Develop methods for calculating 1/4 of a quantity;

- Determine the amount "left over" when 1/4 is removed.

In *Lesson 3*, the fraction 3/4 is the focus, and students

- Develop methods for calculating 3/4 of a quantity;

- Connect division and multiplication with finding 3/4 of a quantity.

In *Lesson 4*, the three benchmarks serve as referents between which other fractions exist. Students

- Compare fractions involving numbers up to 1,000 to determine where they are located in relationship to the benchmarks (1/2, 1/4, or 3/4).

In *Lessons 5* and *6*, the decimal 0.1 (.1) is introduced. Students

- Find one-tenth of a quantity;

- Identify multiple ways of representing one-tenth (1/10, 0.1, and 10%) and relate them to visual models.

Assessments

Assessment should be the servant of teaching and learning (Beyond Arithmetic, 1995, p. 84).

Using Benchmarks: Fractions, Decimals, and Percents opens and closes with assessment. In both cases, the *Teacher Book* provides multiple ways to gauge what students know. There are also tools for ongoing assessment in each lesson. These components are described next.

Opening the Unit

This session provides an opportunity to welcome students and to evaluate students' knowledge of benchmark fractions, decimals, and percents.

Making a Mind Map: This provides evidence of students' ideas and experiences related to fractions, decimals, and percents.

I Will Show You 1/2!: Students show 1/2 and discuss methods for finding 1/2.

Initial Assessment: The session closes with a written assessment that asks students what they know about the various benchmark fractions (1/2, 1/4, and 3/4) and the benchmark decimal 0.1 and asks them to compare other fractions to the benchmarks. They then share their thinking about a "best deal" problem involving pricing for a 1/2-liter and a full-liter bottle of water. The assessment helps you determine where to begin and on what to concentrate in the lessons that follow. However, before students start the tasks, they first indicate how capable they feel of completing each problem by checking off "Can do," "Don't know how," or "Not sure." We recommend that you ask them to complete the tasks that they feel confident they can do. Checked against the *Initial Assessment Checklist*, the *Initial Assessment* will indicate which lessons will be new material and which lessons will be reviews.

The purpose of the opening session is to introduce students to the content of the unit and to give you information about their understanding. It is not designed as a teaching lesson, so refrain from using the session as an opportunity to teach all the concepts. The six lessons are designed to help students solidify their grasp of the content.

Closing the Unit

The *Final Assessment* is an opportunity for students to synthesize what they have learned.

Standing Up: This activity starts with the class describing the demographics of a protest crowd using fractions, decimals, and percents and a number-line segment.

Review Session: Students go over all the lessons and skills they recall learning before reviewing their personal work to create a small portfolio.

Final Assessment: Mirroring the *Initial Assessment*, the *Final Assessment* asks students to determine how capable they feel about completing a problem before they attempt it. Students complete the tasks for the final written assessment.

Mind Map: This second Mind Map is compared to the first one created in the opening session as students self-assess the changes in their understanding from the beginning to the end of the unit.

Ongoing Assessment

Much of the work students do will take place in small groups or pairs. This work must be assessed to determine whether students are absorbing the main ideas and to diagnose difficulties, as well as provide more challenging work to students. The *Looking Closely* section of each lesson focuses teachers' attention on objectives and the corresponding observable behavior. As students gain skills, teachers will want to track their progress and communicate observations to them. Each lesson has a chart called *What to Look For in Lesson X* with four dimensions for assessing students' progress:

Concept Development: The student grasps big ideas and technical skills.

Expressive Capacity: The student shows an ability to describe, reason aloud, and explain to others. This is easiest to observe in written work, a record with strong evidence of understanding and misconceptions or errors. However, a student's oral remarks are often a more accurate reflection of what he or she knows.

Use of Tools: The student uses objects, diagrams, number-line segments, arrays, and *x*- and *y*-axes to show and enhance understanding.

Notation Use: The student understands and utilizes notational forms appropriately.

Bearing in mind these dimensions of assessment will help you formulate "next steps" for teaching.

A Final Word

Upon first appearance, the content of this unit might strike you and your students as quite easy, but the simplicity is deceptive. EMPower pilot teachers told us the unit had a lot of "sticking power" for their students, who used their learnings as a basis for success in subsequent mathematics classes. People became more self-assured and less dependent on teacher direction. By taking the time to establish the concepts of part-whole, a portion of an amount, and benchmarks from which to think about other fractions, decimals, and percents, students will lay a foundation that serves them well as they continue to make sense of numbers in their everyday lives.

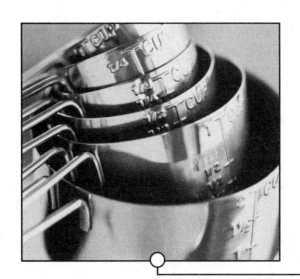

Facilitating Opening the Unit: Using Benchmarks

> *What are the most common fractions?*

Synopsis

In this session, you will discover what students already know about the benchmark fractions 1/2, 1/4, 3/4, and 1/10 and the decimal 0.1. As students work, two ideas about the fraction 1/2 become evident: first, the idea of halving as an action or operation and second, the concept of one-half as the description of a part-whole relationship. By the end of the session, you will have an idea how best to use this unit in your class.

1. The group brainstorms and individual students record what they know about fractions, decimals, and percents.

2. Individuals or pairs of students demonstrate halving by first drawing or acting out half of various amounts and then identifying the part and whole of various amounts.

3. Students show you the notation for one-half that is familiar to them.

4. Students relate one-half to division by two.

5. Students look over an *Initial Assessment* to determine what parts, if any, they feel confident they can complete. Individually or in pairs they complete those parts before reviewing today's learning.

Objectives

- Demonstrate halving in a way that shows an understanding of halves as two equal parts of a whole
- Demonstrate familiarity with notation for half
- Write a fraction to show the part and the whole in various representations
- Calculate half of two-digit numbers
- Demonstrate prior knowledge of the fractions 1/2, 1/4, 3/4, and 1/10 and the decimal 0.1

Materials/Prep

- Calculators (optional)
- Counters such as bingo chips, square-inch tiles, or paper clips
- Graph paper
- Markers
- Masking tape
- Newsprint
- String

Make one copy per student of the *Initial Assessment Checklist* (*Appendices*, p. 93) to record your observations and one copy of the *Class Tally* (*Appendices*, p. 92) to record class responses to assessment problems. Make a copy of the *Initial Assessment* (*Appendices*, p. 87) for each student.

Prepare a *Fractions, Decimals, and Percents* class vocabulary list on a sheet of newsprint to be posted at the front of the class and added to throughout the unit.

Prepare a newsprint drawing or transparency of the Mind Map, p. 2 (save results for later comparisons).

Heads Up!

Allow students to experiment with the concept of "**half**." Offer them the counters as one possible way to show half, but encourage them to represent the fractions as they wish.

For students who do not come up with a way to draw half, suggest they use one of the following shapes to mark one-half.

or

Opening Discussion

Start with a reference to commonly used fractions and why they are so important in everyday life.

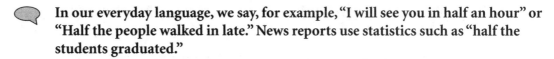 **In our everyday language, we say, for example, "I will see you in half an hour" or "Half the people walked in late." News reports use statistics such as "half the students graduated."**

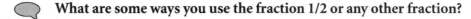 **What are some ways you use the fraction 1/2 or any other fraction?**

Take a few examples from the class, listing the fractions mentioned on the board. Offer students an overview of and purpose for the unit in broad strokes. Tell students that this unit will build their understanding of how **fractions**, **decimals**, and **percents** work and will give them the skills to handle those most commonly used.

By the end of *Opening the Unit*, you should have several artifacts:

- Mind Map (*Activity 1*)
- *I Will Show You 1/2!* (*Activity 2*)
- *Initial Assessment* (at least Problem 4)

Activity 1: Making a Mind Map

The Mind Map provides the first evidence of students' prior knowledge of fractions, decimals, and percents. This part of the session should take no more than 15 minutes.

Fractions, decimals, and percents are everywhere, and you may have some ideas about them. We will make a Mind Map so everyone can record his or her thoughts and impressions about fractions, decimals, and percents.

Start the activity by posting your newsprint or transparency copy of the Mind Map. Ask a few generative questions:

What comes to mind when you think of the words "fractions, decimals, and percents"?

Where do you see fractions, decimals, and percents?

For what purposes do people use these numbers?

Write down a few ideas. Model clustering them, linking related ideas with lines, and then ask students to record their own ideas on p. 2 of the *Student Book*. After a few minutes, ask students to write one or two of their ideas on Post-it® Notes (or, if a transparency is used, to call them out for you to record). Create new clusters as needed on the class Mind Map.

It is interesting to save this product as well as individual Mind Maps to see which attitudes and what knowledge change over the course of the unit.

As terms related to fractions, decimals, and percents arise, start a class vocabulary list on the prepared newsprint sheet. Do not worry about formal, dictionary-style definitions; use what students themselves say. You will want to add and refer to this word list throughout the unit. Students can take notes in the *Vocabulary* sections of their books, starting on p. 101.

Activity 2: I Will Show You 1/2!

Part 1

Refer students to *I Will Show You 1/2!* (*Student Book*, p. 3), and explain the directions:

💬 **Pick something in the room that you can use to show one-half. You must be able to show the class the whole and the part. You may draw or act out the half and the whole amount.**

💬 **Show us how you figured out half of the whole amount.**

💬 **Record your version of one-half with numbers.**

Bring the class together and ask students to share, inviting a variety of examples and methods. Students record examples on the board.

Showing 1/2

Part	Whole	Fraction	Method
4	8	4/8	8÷2=4
36"	72"	36"/72"	36"+36"=72"

Ask in each case:

💬 **What is the part?**

💬 **What is the whole?**

💬 **How did you write the fraction?**

💬 **How did you know it was one-half?**

Ask each group:

💬 **What happens if you total your two halves?**

If the group's two halves do not total the whole, ask how this can be.

Heads Up!

Switch units if necessary; for example, 1/2 cup is also 4 oz./8 oz.

At appropriate times, ask the class:

💬 **What is another way to say, for example, that Cara read one-half of the book?**

Emphasize that one-half can be written as "1/2," "a half," "0.5," or "50%." All are valid ways to represent one-half. Record these representations on the class vocabulary list. Take a few moments to consider the contexts in which each of them is most commonly used.

Synthesizing Ideas

Check to see whether students realize that the amount in one-half will differ depending on the amount in the whole. Indicating students' examples on the board, ask:

💬 **What do all of these fractions have in common?**

💬 **The numbers change, but they are all one-half. Why?**

💬 **Can two halves created from a single thing or things ever be different sizes? How do you know?**

Make a point of distinguishing between everyday life, where one can get the "bigger half" of a sandwich, and mathematical practice, where halves of a whole are always equal in size or number.

Finally, ask the class:

💬 **In general, how do you find one-half of something?**

Reach consensus on some rules for finding one-half, and post them on the vocabulary list. If the following point is not brought up, mention it yourself:

💬 **When you see "one-half," it is a sign to make two groups and find the amount of the parts of one of those groups.**

This may also be a good time to write "1/2," "50%," and "0.5" next to some of the student fraction examples to emphasize that although the notation appears different, they all represent the same amount.

If two-digit numbers have not been mentioned during the discussion, especially odd two-digit numbers, discuss them now. Ask questions such as these:

💬 **Using our rules, what would half of $75 be?**

💬 **How far away from me does my niece live if she is half as far away as my aunt, who is 55 miles away?**

💬 **If two people split the check for a nice dinner that cost $37, how much would each person pay?**

💬 **If the distance from your home to your brother's house were 99 miles, how many miles would you travel before you were halfway there?**

Ask students how they arrived at their answers. At this point, you will have a snapshot of the following:

- Who understands how to find one-half of an amount;
- What methods students use to arrive at an answer (addition, multiplication, or division);
- Who can refer to one-half in a variety of appropriate ways; and
- Who is clear about the need for halves to be of equal size.

Heads Up!

State that in a fraction the bottom number (denominator) tells how many parts make up the total—that is, the whole—and the top number (numerator) tells how many out of the total number of parts are being counted as the fraction.

Part 2 (*Student Book*, p. 4) of this activity can be assigned as homework for those who need or want more practice finding one-half of a total amount. Students again look for patterns for halves between part and whole numbers and state a rule for finding a half.

Activity 3: Initial Assessment

Begin the *Initial Assessment* with a review of the questions. It is recommended that you show the problems on an overhead projector or otherwise display them for the whole class to see. In addition, distribute a copy of the *Initial Assessment* to every student. As a volunteer reads each question, ask the class:

💬 **How many of you think you can do this problem?**

💬 **How many of you think you cannot do it?**

💬 **How many of you are not sure whether you can do it?**

Tally responses on the *Class Tally* (*Appendices*, p. 92). Depending on the class responses, assign only Task 5, some other problems also, or all the problems for students to complete individually. Task 5 can be done in groups or, if few of the students thought they could do it, as a class. Collect any work you assign for later review.

Post replicas of the number lines in Task 5. Review how students found half of each number and located it on the number line. This work is crucial preparation for the next class. Do not skip it.

Use the *Initial Assessment Checklist* (*Appendices*, p. 93) to keep track of individual progress on the assessment.

Heads Up!

A review of student work on all three activities will guide your decisions about proceeding with the unit. Some classes may benefit from more work with halves (see pp. 7–22 in *Lesson 1*); some classes will appear extremely fluent with halves and quarters, so starting with the fraction 3/4 would be a better choice. Where you start depends on the needs of your class.

Summary Discussion

Ask students to record their thoughts in *Reflections* (*Student Book*, p. 103). Then ask:

Benchmarks

 What stood out for you?

 What are you still curious about?

Ask students:

 You demonstrated finding half, and you showed half an amount. What can you say about half that is true in all situations?

Take statements from volunteers, and if the following points are not brought up, mention them yourself.

- Each display for one-half had two parts, and both parts were the same size and/or had the same number of subparts.

- One-half can be shown in many different ways, depending on the whole.

- Half describes the relationship of a part or parts to a whole. Half does not always have the same value; half of 8 is not equal to half of 15.

Looking Closely

Observe whether students are able to

Demonstrate halving in a way that shows an understanding of halves as two equal parts of a whole

Do students' representations demonstrate understanding of halving? When students show one-half, their actions will be key to understanding their concept of a half. Look for cutting, breaking, splitting, or dealing into two *equal* parts. Ask students to explain how their representations show one-half, and as they do, highlight the notion of a whole being divided into two parts.

Demonstrate familiarity with notation for half

Do students recognize that there is more than one right way to write a half? Clearly the fact that the value of a half and the way to write it can vary is unsettling to some students. Point out that the notation allows for many right answers, depending on the context. Take time to consider different contexts for the different representations of one-half. You might correctly report that 37 out of 74 students passed a test, but in some circumstances (particularly math tests!), you would want to emphasize that 37/74 equaled half the students. If you were using a pie chart, you would show 50% of the students passing.

Write a fraction to show the part and the whole in various representations

Can students find the part and the whole? Some objects and situations lend themselves to halving better than others. Ask how to quantify one-half of an amount if an exact measurement is necessary. Cover half of a set of objects (e.g., paper clips), and ask students how many they think are in the other half. Uncover them to determine whether the two halves are equal in size.

Students may have difficulty partitioning a unit into its parts, for example, a book of 170 pages. It is helpful to use labels: 85 pages read (part, or numerator)/170 pages of the book (whole, or denominator). Similarly, students may find it easy to estimate half a surface (such as a door, floor, or window) but not think to measure it with a single unit (such as inches or feet) to create the components of a fraction.

Calculate half of two-digit numbers

Can students find half of two-digit even and odd numbers? Note which numbers give students difficulty. Suggest they use strategies such as doubling to check their guesses. Show them how to use even numbers that can easily be halved to find halves of odd numbers. For example, to find half of 41 people in a cafeteria, they can begin by finding half of 40, which is 20; the remainder will be one person— who cannot be cut in half! An exact half can more easily be found for $41.00: $20.50.

Demonstrate prior knowledge of the fractions 1/2, 1/4, 3/4, and 1/10 and the decimal 0.1

The *Initial Assessment* reveals what students know as well as what they do not know or feel confident about in terms of benchmark fractions and decimals. Throughout the unit, students will encounter these terms and develop an understanding of them. Do not push for full understanding in this session.

WHAT TO LOOK FOR IN *OPENING THE UNIT*	WHO STANDS OUT? (LIST STUDENTS' INITIALS)			NOTES FOR NEXT STEPS
	STRONG	ADEQUATE	NEEDS WORK	
Concept Development • Is able to halve (mark a surface to show two equal parts or divide a group into two equal parts) • Recognizes the part and whole in a variety of situations • Connects dividing or splitting actions with finding a half of something (denominator indicates number of parts into which the whole is divided)				
Expressive Capacity • Uses the terms "part" and "whole" appropriately				
Notation Use • Recognizes different notation for one-half • Connects notation with the appropriate situations				

Rationale

This is an assessment session; you want to get an idea of what your students already know about fractions, decimals, and percents by listening to their comments, explanations, and interpretations. You will use this information to make instructional decisions about which lessons to use with your class. Demonstrating one-half is a welcoming introduction for students with varied backgrounds, many of whom describe fractions as the "fall-apart" point for them in their mathematics experience.

Math Background

Fractions are sometimes confusing to people. The idea that half can stand for many different values—depending on the whole—is tricky. Focus on the part-whole relationship (10 student *out of* 20 students), as opposed to a part-part relationship, (one tutor *for* two students). All of the lessons in *Benchmark Fractions, Decimals, and Percents* will refer to a half as indicating a part-whole relationship and as a sign to divide a total into two equal parts.

However, it is important to remember that most people have an intuitive sense of half, regardless of their mathematics education. Often those who rely on intuitive knowledge of half benefit from questions that make the math more explicit, such as, "What did you do to make halves? How many sections, parts, or pieces did you create when you made halves? How many of those pieces constitute one-half of the whole?"

Facilitation

As you listen and watch, take notes using the *Initial Assessment Checklist* (*Appendices*, p. 93) to keep track of each student's comprehension. Some will have a thorough understanding of half; others will not. Some will easily connect equivalent percents and decimals with appropriate contexts; others will not. Some will be able to locate a halfway mark on a surface but experience difficulty in quantifying that measurement. Encourage students to articulate their reasoning to you, to each other, and to the class. In doing so, you are establishing a climate for sharing ideas.

Making the Lesson Easier

Give students 10 paper clips, a stack of six books, or a pile of eight pieces of paper, and ask them to show you half. Help them verbalize how they determine a half. Once students are clear that the halving process involves dividing one whole into two equal parts, and that one-half is one *out of* those two parts, continue to practice with sets of objects or shapes (e.g., strips of paper) that can easily be halved. When you think students are ready to find half of an odd number, use pieces of paper or index cards as manipulatives so the "one left over" can be cut in half to create a visual image.

Money can and should be used when thinking about fractions, decimals, and percents. However, experience has shown us that although students know that 50 cents is half a dollar, they do not necessarily recognize that we are talking about a *part* consisting of 50 cents out of a *whole* 100 cents that make up a dollar. Similarly, they often do not equate $0.50 with 50/100ths or 5/10ths. Money is often the automatic reference for students; they will not necessarily bring up other measurements and images that can also help them understand fractions. Encouraging them to visualize fractions in other ways will help them with fractions that do not easily relate to money.

On many occasions, students may draw a circle. However, shapes similar to the following ones will be more useful for comparisons.

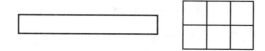

Making the Lesson Harder

When a student has already shown half in several ways, ask him or her to find half a kilo, a pound, a mile, and half of other measurements. Ask how one measures half a circle. Let the student try finding half of a large number, such as 8,008,278, the population of New York City (2000 census, http://www.ci.nyc.ny.us/html/dcp/html/census/pop2000.html).

Introduce the concept of one-half of one-half (one-quarter) by asking a question such as the following:

 When is a half not a half? When the whole is a part of something. For instance, after Jason's birthday party, half the cake was left over. Aunt Sally gave half the leftover cake to the birthday boy to take home. What part of the whole cake did Aunt Sally keep for herself?

Being asked to choose something to demonstrate one-half allows students the freedom to focus on what is meaningful to them.

The following list represents ways individuals in one class chose to demonstrate one-half.

- Livia drew lines across the middles of a 3-D cylinder and a 2-D circle.

- Caleb wrote down "100, 50%, and 0.5."

- Jill wrote that half a day was 12/24, and half a 500-mg pill was 250 mg.

- Marie split a drawing of an apple into two pieces.

- Van drew 10 socks and shaded five.

- Dave said that half the alphabet is 13/26 letters; half the senators are 50.

On the board, students showed the following:

- Half a 10-piece chocolate bar shaded

- A necklace with the sign "50% sale—Whole is $200.00; part is $100.00"

- A baby bottle halfway full, marked "She drank half the bottle."

Marilyn Moses, observed by Marilyn Matzko
Brockton Adult Education Center, Brockton, MA

Even an apparently simple notion can lead to some revelatory moments for students. In this class, talk of "one-half" led to one student's questions about the connection to 0.5 and her paycheck. Along the way, another student learned a way to find half a group of objects.

The class had many manipulatives available—cubes, pennies, pencils, calculators, etc. Students were to pick some and find the whole and the half.

As they worked, the students talked about "whole" and "half" and how they determined a half.

- 38 orange blocks, half is 19—counted them.

- 28 white cubes, half is 14—divided by two.

- Started with 15 calculators, got rid of one, left with 14, found half to be seven—put them into two equal piles.

- 20 cubes, half was 10—made one pile of green, one pile of orange, each with 10.

- 26 blocks—one long array—started by making five piles; with some prodding, made two and found 13 in each. ("I didn't think of it that way before.")

Then Rosa said, "That 'point five'—I've always wondered about it. In my paycheck, they write something about overtime being 1.5... what is that? Why do I get $17.25?" The teacher wrote out her problem and together the group solved it:

"I get $11.50 an hour... so half that is $5.75 (the class chimed in the answer) and so... $11.50 + $5.75 = $17.25. Wow," said Rosa, "I never knew how they got that number, but now I see it."

Carol Kolenik, observed by Myriam Steinback
Harvard Bridge to Learning and Literacy, Cambridge, MA

1

More Than, Less Than, or Equal to One-Half?

> *Where's the halfway mark?*

Synopsis

This lesson makes explicit how to set up a fraction by finding the number of parts in the whole and using that number for the denominator. This is the first lesson that asks students to compare a fractional amount to a benchmark fraction—1/2.

1. The whole class completes a doubling and halving warm-up exercise.

2. Student pairs visit Fraction Stations to identify the part and whole in various situations and to compare that fraction to the benchmark 1/2. If more practice is needed finding halves, students work on practices.

3. The class identifies a number to represent the whole at each station.

4. Student pairs further practice identifying the part, setting up a fraction, and then comparing the fraction to the benchmark 1/2.

5. The whole class brainstorms a list of ideas to remember, and individuals write about these in *Reflections* (*Student Book*, p. 103).

Objectives

- Identify the part and the whole in various cases
- Determine whether a fractional amount is more than, less than, or equal to 1/2
- State the fraction that represents the whole for any case

Materials/Prep

Prepare five Fraction Stations that communicate the idea of a total and some part of it. The example at Station 1 will be a page from a monthly calendar with 16 days crossed out. Some other Fraction Station suggestions are a box of large and small paper clips; a game board like Monopoly with a piece positioned a few squares from the starting point; a phone book with a bookmark at the halfway point; a sheet for a fund-raising walk with 19 out of 36 lines filled in with pledges; a prototype bill with a check for less than half the amount due; and a yardstick marked at 20 inches.

Heads Up!

Throughout this lesson and the practices, the terms "1/2," "0.5," and "50%" will be used interchangeably so students learn how to recognize and when to use each.

Opening Discussion

Review the main ideas about halves by asking:

💬 **What do you do to find one-half of something?** (Split it into two, divide by two, etc.)

💬 **What are some mathematical terms for one-half?** (1/2, 0.5, 50%)

💬 **What is an example of a half?**

Conduct a quick warm-up exercise emphasizing mental math—halving and doubling; or, if students appear to need more practice, refer them to pp. 12–20, *Student Book*, to complete the practices before proceeding.

💬 **It is useful to picture the amount of a fraction by comparing it to a half.**

💬 **Is the fraction more than, less than, or equal to one-half?**

Offer examples that require students to halve an amount or to determine the whole, given a half. Use numbers that are easily divisible by two. Some examples follow:

- Out of 100 parents, half attended the school committee meeting.
- The town clerk raised the cost of fishing licenses to $25. Last year they were half that price.
- Isaiah bench-pressed 120 pounds, setting a personal record. However, this is only half the weight he wants to be able to lift.
- Willard's is having a 50%-off sale. Jackets are now selling for $25.

Heads Up!

The more current the data, the better. Use *local* news information to frame your examples, if possible.

Then explain the idea of a **benchmark** fraction.

> **One-half is a benchmark fraction, just as 10 and 100 are benchmark numbers. Benchmarks are points of reference used for comparison.**

> **All of the fractions discussed in this unit are benchmark fractions commonly used to compare quantities.**

Add "benchmark fraction" to the class vocabulary list.

Introduce the following problem:

> A new building is going up in my neighborhood. At first more than half the apartments were supposed to be affordable housing units. Now people are saying that 20 of the 45 apartments will be rent-controlled. I wonder, is that really so many? Is it more than half? Less than half?

> **What are some different ways you could figure this out?**

Keep the focus of the discussion on different ways to find the answer. Make sure students are exposed to at least three or four approaches. Some examples follow:

- *An approach based on reasoning about doubling*, such as 20 units multiplied by two are 40 units—less than half

- *An approach based on division*, such as half of 45 is 22 1/2; or 45 divided by 2 is 22.5; or 40 ÷ 2 = 20 and 5 ÷ 2 = 2 1/2

- *A diagramming approach* with representative amounts:

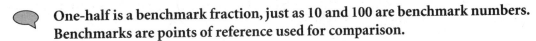

- *A graphing approach*:

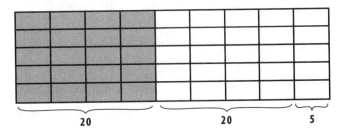

- *A number line approach*:

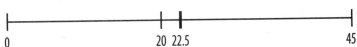

Heads Up!

Students are called upon to use number lines throughout this lesson and the practices. Take time to review reading and marking number lines.

Do a quick survey among students.

💬 **Which way makes the most sense to you? Why?**

Tell students:

💬 **Any of these methods can help you solve problems involving the fraction 1/2. Knowing a few of them will allow you to choose one that works for you and will provide some ideas if you get stuck.**

🌀 Activity 1: Stations—Comparing Fractions to 1/2

Review directions *in Student Book,* p. 8. Complete the first example as a class. Ask students:

💬 **Where do I find the number for the *part*? For the *whole*?**

💬 **What fraction of this month is crossed out?**

💬 **Is that fraction more than, less than, or equal to 1/2? How do you know?**

Listen to students' explanations, and relate them to the methods described earlier, especially the use of operations and the number line. Complete the table for the calendar.

Ask:

💬 **What fraction of this month is *not* crossed out? How did you determine that?**

💬 **Is that fraction more than, less than, or equal to 1/2? How do you know?**

Tell student pairs to visit each station to complete their tables. Listen to how students reach conclusions so you can summarize later and address any questions that arose.

Post a copy of the table on the board. Invite pairs to complete the table and explain how they determined answers. Have students show their reasoning on a number line segment with 0 at one end (e.g., 0/30); the whole amount at the other end (e.g., 30/30); the halfway point (e.g., 15/30); and the actual fraction represented (e.g., 16/30).

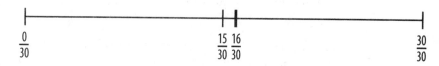

Once everyone has agreed on the answers, return to the idea of writing a fraction to represent the whole.

💬 **For each station, how would you write a fraction that represents the whole?**

Help students articulate that a fraction representing a whole always has the same top and bottom numbers, that is, the same number of parts being counted as there are in the whole. Elicit a few quick examples from students to help cement the notion of a fraction showing the whole. Then ask:

💬 **What do you change to write the fraction for one-half? How do you change it? How do you know?**

◎ Activity 2: Is It Half?

Divide the class into three groups for further practice. Ask each group to try two of the problems from *Is It Half?* (*Student Book*, p. 9) and to explain the solutions in two ways. Encourage students to use visual representations, bingo chips, or paper clips for one of their methods so it will be easy to retrace their steps later.

When all the groups have finished, call the class together to share solutions and strategies. As needed, prompt discussion with questions such as the following:

💬 **What is the whole? What are the parts?**

💬 **How did pictures help you think about this problem? What different pictures did others use?**

💬 **Who thought about it in a different way?**

Summary Discussion

Brainstorm and record a list of points to remember, e.g., finding the whole, dividing by two, and writing a fraction with the number for the parts being counted recorded above the number for the whole, or all the parts. Students enter one or more ideas in *Reflections* (*Student Book*, p. 103).

Benchmarks

◎ Practice

Half the Size, p. 12
For visual practice finding one-half.

Why Is 50% a Half?, p. 14

Find Half of It, p.15

Choose an Amount, p. 16

More "Is It 1/2?" Problems, p. 17
For practice comparing fractions to 1/2, as well as writing fractions for wholes, halves, and existing amounts.

What Is the Whole?, p. 18
For practice finding the whole, given the half, and writing fractions for wholes.

Which Is Larger?, p. 20
The concept of comparing fractions against the benchmark 1/2 is extended to allow the comparison of pairs of fractions.

Extension

Extension: Half a Million?, p. 21
For practice comparing fractions to 1/2 using graph data.

Test Practice

Test Practice, p. 23

Heads Up!

A Test Practice is included in every lesson, always in the same format, with five multiple choice items and one response item. If you wish, photocopy accompanying Test Practice Answer Sheets (Blackline Master 7) that are layed out in the GED response format

Looking Closely

Observe whether students are able to

Identify the part and the whole in various cases

As students are counting, arranging objects, or making their own drawings, ask about the part and the whole. Some students will think of a fraction as a ratio between two parts, for example, the number of crossed-out days on a calendar compared to the number that are blank. They might write "16/14" or "14/16." Affirm that these fractions do describe aspects of the situation, but ask them to identify the whole. When they focus on the relationship between the part and the whole, they will be able to compare the fraction to the benchmark 1/2.

Determine whether a fractional amount is more than, less than, or equal to one-half

Do students easily find the fraction representing 1/2? Are they able to compare the fraction representing the part to the benchmark 1/2? Finding 1/2 is the first step in comparison. Students may have difficulty mentally dividing numbers, especially larger, unwieldy numbers. Once they know they need to divide by two, a calculator may prove useful. Help students decompose (break apart) numbers. For instance, if they want to find 1/2 of 45, ask them to find 1/2 of 40 and then 1/2 of 5. Practice the language of comparison as well. For example, "The fraction 7/18 shows 7 parts. The 1/2 fraction would have 9/18, which is more than 7/18, so 7/18 is less than 1/2."

If comparing a fraction to a 1/2 (or 50%) is easy, ask students to estimate the percent they think the fractional amount represents. Check their estimates and ask students to explain how they arrived at them. A good assignment for these students might be to create a combination of circle graphs to show percents, and rectangles or number lines to show the fractions. Students with a strong sense of percents can estimate answers in percents on practice sheets.

State the fraction that represents the whole for any case

Do students understand that a fraction can represent a whole as well as a part of something? Help students see that the number of parts counted can equal the total number of parts in an object. Choose an object composed of a small number of items—a pack of gum, for instance. Show the pack to students several times, each time with one more piece missing. Ask: "What fraction represents the missing part of the pack?" Continue until the pack is empty. This will help students see the logic of the notation representing a whole. Point out that the term "whole pack" does not indicate the number of pieces in the pack; however, a fraction like 7/7 or 5/5 tells the number of pieces in a whole pack *and* the number of pieces missing— all of them.

It is not yet necessary for students to connect that the part they are counting and the part remaining equal one whole when added together. However, for some students this connection helps make sense of writing the fraction for one whole— 2/5 of the pieces of gum are missing; 3/5 of the pieces are left. So a whole package must have 5/5 pieces because the parts must equal one whole, just as halves must add up to equal one whole.

WHAT TO LOOK FOR IN *LESSON 1*	WHO STANDS OUT? (LIST STUDENTS' INITIALS)			NOTES FOR NEXT STEPS
	STRONG	ADEQUATE	NEEDS WORK	
Concept Development • Understands "part" and "whole" • Understands whole fractions • Uses 1/2, 0.5, and 50%				
Expressive Capacity • Uses terms for one-half in appropriate contexts				
Use of Tools • Uses manipulatives to determine and demonstrate halves • Uses diagrams to determine and demonstrate halves • Uses a number line to determine and demonstrate halves				

Rationale

Reports and articles often use benchmark fractions and percents to communicate statistics. Students will easily interpret such data if they are able to distinguish between the part and the whole. They will also more easily generate meaningful statements about situations they encounter at work, at home, or in their communities.

Math Background

According to the National Council of Teachers of Mathematics (NCTM), students "should develop strategies for ordering and comparing fractions, often using benchmarks such as 1/2 and 1" (*Principles and Standards*, 2000, p.150). The use of these benchmarks can help students think about questions such as, "Which is larger, 2/5 or 5/8?" Those who can reason that 2/5 is less than 1/2 because 2 1/2 is half of 5, and 5/8 is more than 1/2 because 4 is half of 8 develop a conceptual basis for number-crunching work involving common denominators and learn to rely on that reasoning. Furthermore, benchmarks help students learn to estimate totals by thinking about whether numbers are close to a whole or a half and, eventually, whether they are close to 1/4 or 3/4.

Facilitation

Making the Lesson Easier

Spend more time finding a half before introducing comparisons. Share strategies such as anticipating the last digit to be five if the original number ends in zero. Assign *Half the Size*, p. 12; *Why Is 50% a Half?*, p. 14, *More "Is It 1/2?" Problems*, p. 17, and *Find Half of It*, p. 15 (all are practices in the *Student Book*).

Making the Lesson Harder

Change the numbers to three-digit numbers or unwieldy numbers. Offer students calculators to check their answers. Make sure they know which number to enter first if they are using the division key. Encourage students to estimate a percent to match the fractional amount (more than, less than, or equal to 50%?). Assign *Extension: Half a Million?* (*Student Book*, p. 21).

Adults bring different background knowledge and preferences for problem solving to math classes. In the following student work samples, you will see that some students rely on words, while others draw diagrams; and some diagrams are more evocative than others. Consider what you might suggest to students to make their diagrams clearer.

The problem: "Sherri dropped a box of 80 crackers. She took them all out and counted 60 broken crackers. The number of broken crackers was more than 1/2 the box, less than 1/2 the box, or 1/2 the whole box."

Alan's diagram with its equal rows of crackers clearly demonstrates the answer: more than 1/2. He uses numbers to support the information in the diagram.

Tenzin's reliance on numbers shows greater abstraction. However, it is not clear how he arrived at some of the fractions he accurately ascribes to the broken and unbroken crackers.

Celine relied on reasoning with halves to reach her answer. She already knows that half of a half equals one-fourth.

whole = 80
1/2 = 40
1/4 = 20

Judy Hikes
Harvard Bridge to Learning and Literacy, Cambridge, MA

Lora also relies on reasoning with halves to find the answer but expresses herself verbally as well as quantitatively.

> Number 40 is half of the whole quantity, but she broke 60, so it is more than 1/2 the quantity.

K.B.
LaGuardia Community College, Long Island City, NY

A review of homework from this lesson, Practice: Find Half of It, *resulted in the following conversation in which the teacher observer guides the learner. She asks questions that help the student tap into his reasoning and number skills to determine half of 72 laps, or one mile, of swimming. Her introduction of a second example helps the student identify a useful strategy for finding half of unfamiliar numbers: Start with part of the number that is close to it, but familiar.*

As Jorge was trying to figure out half of 72, he reasoned:

Half of 7 is 3 1/2, and half of 2 is 1, so the answer is 3 1/2 plus 1—4 1/2.

I asked whether that answer made sense to him. He thought about it and said that half of 72 could not be 4 1/2 and could not be 45 either, but he did not know how to fix that problem.

Teacher: "How do you know that it can't be 45?"

Jorge: "Because doubling it makes more than 72."

Teacher: "Okay. So if starting with 7 didn't help you, what other number might you start with that could help?"

Jorge: "I don't know."

Teacher: "Would 70 help?"

Jorge: "No, that's not an easy one for me."

Teacher: "If I asked you what is half of 60, would you say that's easy for you?"

Jorge: "Yes! It's 30."

continued on next page

continued from previous page

Teacher: "Okay. So you're at 60, but the problem you have is what?"

Jorge: "Seventy-two laps."

Teacher: "Okay. How does knowing 60 help you?"

Jorge: "From 60 to 72 it's 12."

Teacher: "And...?"

Jorge: "And I don't know."

Teacher: "So, half of 60 is 30, but you still have 12 more."

Jorge: "Yes, and half of 12 is 6."

Teacher: "So...?"

Jorge: "Hmmm."

Teacher: "So half of 72 is?"

Jorge: "Thirty and 6. Oh! 36!"

Teacher: "Yes, does that make sense?"

Jorge: "Yes, because I can see that two 36's make 72."

Teacher: "If the number were 98, what could you use to find half?"

Jorge: "Eighty and go from there."

Another student: "But you can also use 100 and go backward."

Myriam Steinback, Teacher Observer
Harvard Bridge to Learning and Literacy, Cambridge, MA

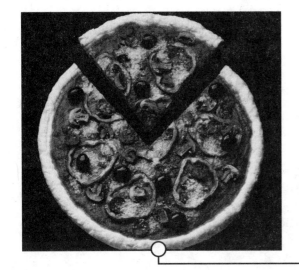

Half of a Half

> *How do you recognize a quarter?*

Synopsis

This lesson builds on students' intuitive knowledge of half and extends it to construct meaning for one-fourth. The concept of a fraction indicating the relationship between part and whole is again emphasized, as is the act of finding one-fourth of a given amount.

1. The class shows one-fourth, solves a problem finding one-fourth, and discusses strategies and synonymous terms.

2. In pairs, students find amounts equal to one-quarter of something wasted or used, defining the leftover amount as well. Pairs also determine the whole of an amount, given one-quarter of it.

3. Pairs test various numbers for the whole and parts of different things to make true statistics involving quarters.

4. The class discusses and individuals write about today's learning.

Objectives

* Find one-fourth of a quantity using multiple strategies, including finding half of half or dividing by four

* Determine the whole and three-fourths of a quantity when one-fourth of the quantity is known

Materials/Prep

- Colored markers
- Counters in different colors
- Graph paper
- Newsprint
- Paper clips
- Snap cubes or other items that learners can use to visualize and represent fractions

On newsprint, draw a large rectangle and a group of 12 apples or stars to use in the *Opening Discussion*.

Opening Discussion

You want to know whether students have ways to find a fourth of a quantity and the remainder of that quantity and whether they have knowledge of different terms for one-fourth. To discover student's conceptions of one-fourth, pose a problem such as the following:

> **Yesterday I was waiting in line at the post office, where *one-fourth* of the people had packages to mail. There were eight people in line. How many had packages?**

Students share solution strategies. Invite other ways of solving the problem until reasoning and visual strategies are shared for the following:

- Halving a half
- Dividing by four
- Diagramming
- Using a number line

Summarize for students by connecting visual representations to part-whole language.

> **One-half indicates one out of two equal groups. One-fourth signifies one out of four equal groups.**

> **How do you get four equal groups? You can divide by four, or you can find half and then divide each half into halves.**

Focus on the whole. Ask:

> **How do you write the fraction to show the whole for four groups?** (4/4) **How do you know?**

> **What fraction represents the whole group of people in line at the post office?** (8/8)

Explain that this lesson involves finding one-fourth of different quantities and also the part that remains out of the whole after one-fourth is accounted for.

> **For instance, in the post-office line there were eight people, and one-fourth of the people, or two out of eight, were mailing packages. How many were not mailing packages?**

Connect this concept to previous visual and reasoning strategies. Then write on the board the following sentence:

One-fourth of the people had packages.

Ask:

💬 **What is another way to say "one-fourth"?**

Add the term "one-fourth" with its synonyms (a quarter, 1/4, 0.25, and 25%) to the class vocabulary list. Reinforce the relationship between one-fourth and one-quarter by introducing a set of words, such as "quart, quadruplets, quarter-pounder, quartet," etc., and asking what all these words have in common. (All relate to the number four.)

Make the connection between finding 50% of a number and finding 25% of the same number.

💬 **We have said one-fourth is half of half. Fifty percent is half of 100%, or the whole; 25% is half of the half, or half of 50%.**

Provide an opportunity to practice the material just covered. Post your newsprint samples of a rectangle and apples or stars. Ask:

💬 **Who can show one-fourth of the rectangle? Who can show one-fourth of the apples (or stars)?**

💬 **What is the whole; what are the parts?**

💬 **How do you know that you have found one-fourth, or 25%?**

💬 **What is the fraction for the whole in each case?**

Remind students that they can call the parts either "quarters" or "fourths" and that the fraction is written the same way in both cases—1/4.

Ask students to look around the classroom to find a few more examples of one-fourth.

🌀 Activity 1: 1/4 Wasted

Review directions for *1/4 Wasted* (*Student Book*, p. 26), where students find one-fourth of an amount wasted or used and the amount remaining. Suggest that students work in pairs.

Notice the strategies students use to solve problems. Encourage the use of reasoning as well as visual approaches.

Heads Up!

The use of "2.5" and "6.5" may baffle some students. Remind students to check the vocabulary list for a definition of "half" and to rewrite the numbers with fractions if that is helpful.

After about 15 minutes, gather the class together to share approaches.

Begin with Problems 1 and 2. Invite students to record their approaches on the board or on newsprint. Prompt with questions such as

How did you find one-fourth? Did anyone start by finding half? Show us how you went from finding half to finding one-fourth.

Did anyone begin with dividing by four? Why did you do that? Show us what you did next.

How did you show your answer for Problem 1a? For Problem 2c?

Finish discussion on the first two problems by asking students to give fractions for each problem that show

- The part wasted;
- The part left;
- The whole.

Continue with Problems 3–5. Ask:

How did you find the total when you knew the part? Who did it differently?

Summarize the methods and then ask:

How did you show your answer for Problem 3b? For Problem 4a?

Follow up by saying:

What did you learn as you found the different fourths?

Students may respond to this question affectively: "I found it was hard to . . ." Or they may respond mathematically: "I found that some numbers divided evenly by four, but some did not"; or "I found that the bigger the number, the bigger one-fourth of it was."

Refer to the parts and the whole if students do not. Check for understanding of one-fourth as a relative amount.

So you are telling me that one-fourth is sometimes two, sometimes 10, and sometimes 25. In the next activity, we will consider how to find a fourth of a total amount.

Activity 2: Is It Really a Quarter?

Review directions for *Is It Really a Quarter?* (*Student Book*, p. 28). Assign either Headline 1, 2, or 3 to each pair of students. Ask pairs to read their headline or statistic. The references do not point to specific numbers, so the goal is for students first to explain the significance of the statistic by inventing a total number or a number that represents a quarter of an imaginary total and then to figure out the complementary number. Do one example together as a class.

One Quarter of All Teenagers Polled Have Never Smoked

Number Polled _____ $\frac{1}{4}$ Never Smoked _____

Ask students:

 How many students might have been polled?

 For that number of students polled, how many would have said they have never smoked?

Take several examples for the number polled. Then figure out one-quarter of each amount—the number of students that would never have smoked.

Heads Up!

It is important for students to see that some numbers (like 125) do not divide evenly by four and therefore do not work when referring to people (the remainder, one person, cannot be divided into parts). You might also want to talk about the significance of numbers in a newspaper report. A poll of only eight people, for instance, is not necessarily newsworthy.

Together script a brief paragraph with a graphic demonstration (a number line, diagram, array, or graph) that relates the supporting numbers and information for the polling headline. Then allow pairs about 10 minutes to work on their problems for *Activity 2*.

As pairs conclude their work, they share their results with others who worked from the same headline prompt. Student pairs check each other's math, diagrams or number lines, and language for accuracy. They also make suggestions for improvements. Several pairs post their work on the board for all to read, and they present their data as if they were newscasters.

Consider the differences between the various tasks.

Close the activity by charting the part-whole, whole fraction, and 1/4 fraction data from everyone's work.

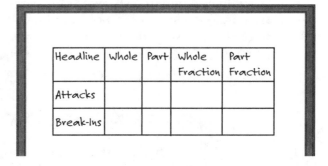

How can you check everyone's *one-quarter* fractions to see whether they are each really a quarter?

Summary Discussion

Post the fraction "1/4" on the board. Ask students what they learned about that fraction today.

As a class or individually, students complete the sentence stem on p. 103, *Reflections* (*Student Book*): "True things to remember about fourths." Prompt their reflections with your own list.

These were some of the things that I heard you say:

- **To find one-fourth, divide by four.**
- **To find the amount left over after one-fourth is accounted for, subtract one-fourth from the whole.**
- **To find the whole when you know one-fourth, multiply the "part" number of the fraction by four.**

Practice

What Makes It a Quarter?, p. 30
A 100-square grid marked as pennies prompts students to consider why the shaded fourth is a quarter, or 25%.

Show Me 1/4!, p. 31
For practice finding one-fourth with visual examples.

1/4 Measurements, p. 33
For practice finding one-fourth of various measurements.

How Many, How Far?, p. 35
For practice solving problems and creating diagrams.

Comparing Fractions to 1/4, p. 39
For practice stating parts, wholes, fractions, and comparing fractions to one-fourth.

 **Extension**

Which Is Larger?, p. 40
A challenge to compare fractions using knowledge about finding one-fourth and/or one-half.

 Test Practice

Test Practice, p. 41

 Looking Closely

Observe whether students are better able to

Find one-fourth of a quantity using multiple strategies, including finding half of half or dividing by four

How do students explain finding fourths? If "half of a half" does not make sense to them, help them articulate the idea of four parts using their own words. Dividing by four is one way, and this will work well for students comfortable with division or with using a calculator. However, in some situations the answer will contain a decimal.

Check whether students use what they know about half to find one-fourth visually or with objects. Assist students in making a visual representation for half and then dividing by two. If they are starting with a new drawing or a new set of objects, for example, encourage them to think about how the two parts could become four. A shape similar to this one

becomes:

Folding a strip of paper in half and then into fourths is helpful. Objects can be divided among the sections to connect the area model of fractions with fractions of discrete numbers. Dividing by two and by two again will help some students keep the meaning of the parts intact.

Encourage students to try multiple strategies so they have ways to check their work, new ways to approach a problem if they get stuck, and some conceptual connections as they encounter more complex fractions.

Determine the whole and three-fourths of a quantity when one-quarter of the quantity is known

In this lesson, students identify three-fourths only as the "leftover" amount after one-fourth is wasted or used. Finding three-fourths of a number and recognizing a fraction as three-fourths are *Lesson 3*'s focus. Determining the amount left over when one-fourth is taken away is a two-step process. The use of objects or shapes partitioned into fourths can help students see that when one-fourth is used up, removed, or subtracted, the remaining amount is three-quarters of the total original amount. Accompany demonstrations with notation to outline computational steps taken to find the amount left over.

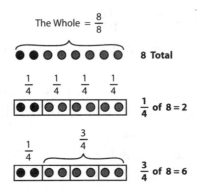

When determining the whole, given one-fourth of it, students may benefit from a reminder of the process used when one-half is known. With halves, they doubled the number. When you discuss fourths, or quarters, the use of a partitioned rectangle can again be helpful. Start with several objects in the first one-fourth of the rectangle. Ask how many would be needed to fill the remaining fourths.

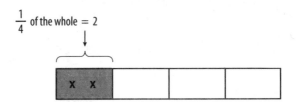

Continue by adding notation to the diagram until students understand that if they know one-fourth, they can add that amount four times or multiply that amount by four to determine the number in the whole.

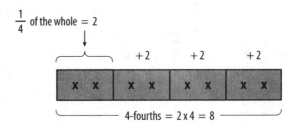

WHAT TO LOOK FOR IN *LESSON 2*	WHO STANDS OUT? (LIST STUDENTS' INITIALS)			NOTES FOR NEXT STEPS
	STRONG	ADEQUATE	NEEDS WORK	
Concept Development • Recognizes the relationship between one-half and one-quarter • Determines one-quarter of a quantity • Determines a whole quantity, given one-quarter of it • Recognizes relationship between one-quarter and three-quarters • Uses 3/4				
Expressive Capacity • Uses one-fourth and one-quarter interchangeably				
Use of Tools • Uses manipulatives to find and demonstrate one-fourth • Uses diagrams to find and demonstrate one-fourth • Uses number lines to find and demonstrate one-fourth				
Notation Use • Writes fractions for the part and the whole • Uses 1/4, 0.25, and 25%				

Rationale

One-fourth is a natural fraction for students to explore after one-half because of the relation between the two fractions. One-fourth is half of one-half. Halves and quarters are also the fractions adults encounter most frequently in measurements of time and length and in the news as statistics; they are benchmarks.

Math Background

The lesson continues with the model of fractions as sectioning amounts larger than one. Avoid introducing linear measurement in which one-quarter inch, for example, is a fixed spot on a measuring tape. The concept of a quarter as a relationship that denotes one of four equal groups will be more useful to students as it reinforces the idea of fractions representing parts and wholes.

Facilitation

Encourage students to report back on their headlines as if they were actually newscasters. They should prepare a three-to-five-sentence report about the numbers. In their roles as TV reporters, they could suggest or create a visual artifact to make their reports clearer or videotape their presentations.

Making the Lesson Easier

Use only numbers divisible by four. Encourage diagrams for all examples, or split up problems so student pairs complete only one set with diagrams and then share their thinking. Make the numbers smaller so that students can more easily represent them with a picture or paper clips.

Making the Lesson Harder

Change the numbers on the activity sheets to include more numbers that are not divisible by four. Tell students to include correct and incorrect numerical data in *Activity 2*, and then ask the class to figure out which statistics are true and which are false.

Students from all classes said that it was easy to find one-fourth of even numbers and hard to find one-fourth of odd numbers. As one student explained when finding one-fourth of three cups in the Brownies problem (How Many, How Far? Student Book, p. 35), "You have to divide one of the cups," and this makes it hard to find one-fourth.

When finding one-fourth of two cups, a student in another class asked, "How can my answer be one-half when I'm looking for one-fourth?" In other words, she wondered how one-fourth could seemingly equal one-half. Distinguishing the operator (one-fourth) and the operated upon (the two-cup measuring cup) challenged this learner. This student might also be troubled by knowing that one-fourth of 16 is the same as one-half of 8 because she would focus on the answer "4" rather than the total amounts involved.

Also, the idea that you can divide a larger number into a smaller number is confounding for some students; thus dividing two cups by four does not seem right. The larger number, as far as they know, is always on the inside of the division box. The teaching work here is to help students understand the need to notate with fractions situations such as four people dividing two apples. No one will get a whole apple; each person will get only a fraction of an apple. In this case, each will get a half an apple. Understanding that the answer is less than one whole object in these cases takes practice.

Shirley drew this picture to represent the 18-block walk of Enrique and his granddaughter Becky. She seemed quite at home using numbers to find her answers as well.

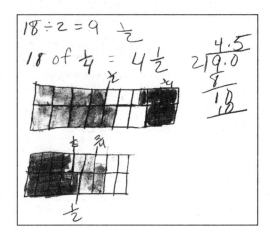

Michelle Brown
Read, Write, Now, Springfield, MA

Tia drew an elaborate and contextually revealing diagram of the 18-block walk taken by Enrique and his granddaughter. She showed 18 streets; however, it is unclear whether she was counting streets or blocks between streets to find her answers. If she had started at 100th Street, her locations for one-fourth and one-half the way would be accurate, but by starting at 101st Street, as she did in the diagram, she will always be one block off. This difference between counting lines and counting spaces between lines frequently surfaces when reading rulers. Tia's answer "on the 9th block" is accurate for the halfway mark; her answer that one-fourth of the way is "between the 4th and 5th block" is also accurate; but a more precise answer would be "at 4 1/2 blocks" and would allow Tia to add her two halves to reconstruct the whole.

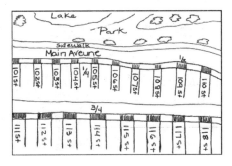

Mark Lance
Borough of Manhattan Community College, New York City, NY

Both of the following students show an understanding of the problem and familiarity with reading a ruler because both count spaces, not lines. The use of numbering in the second diagram makes counting easier and more clearly communicates the problem. Both students' answers were accurate. The first student offered the answers "4.5" and "9" as the 1/4- and 1/2-way marks on the walk, and the second student offered "4 1/2 blocks" and "9 blocks" as his answers.

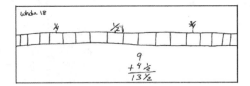

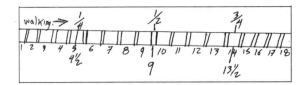

Barbara Tyndall
13/Career Link, Lancaster, PA

Three Out of Four

> *What does three-fourths mean?*

Synopsis

Students build on their knowledge of fourths as they explore the benchmark fraction 3/4.

1. The whole group relates the fraction 3/4 to time, as in quarters of a football or basketball game.

2. The whole class uses the fractions 1/4 and 3/4 to describe a soda pack with a total of 12 cans of soda and outlines various strategies for finding three-fourths.

3. In pairs, students find three-fourths of different amounts.

4. Student pairs compare different quantities to three-fourths.

5. The class discusses rules for finding three-fourths of an amount and important points to remember about three-fourths, especially the significance of the "3" and the "4."

Objectives

- Solve problems by finding three-fourths of a quantity using at least two methods
- Relate finding three-fourths to division and multiplication

Materials/Prep

- Items packaged in 12's or 24's, such as a 12-pack of soda or juice, for use in the *Opening Discussion*

Prepare an enlarged number line and grid for demonstrations of *Activity 1* solutions.

Opening Discussion

Revisit an example or two of finding one-fourth of an amount using packaged items you provide. Review the idea of dividing by four or dividing by two and then two again (half of a half).

Explain that today's lesson involves the benchmark fraction 3/4.

Tell a story such as the following one:

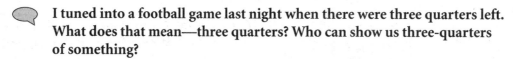 **I tuned into a football game last night when there were three quarters left. What does that mean—three quarters? Who can show us three-quarters of something?**

Allow a few moments for students to generate examples and share demonstrations and diagrams. Ask them:

How do you know you are showing *three-fourths*?

Record students' strategies, asking after each one whether anyone knows another way to show three-fourths. You may hear a few or all of the following:

- Find one-fourth and separate out the rest (or subtract the rest from the whole).
- Find one-fourth and add it three times.
- Divide by four and multiply by three.
- Find half of a half and multiply by three or add up.
- Find one-half and one-fourth and add them.
- Count three of every four.

Return to the problem situation introduced earlier.

So, if the whole football game was an hour long, how many minutes would have been played after three quarters?

Students find the duration for three-quarters of an hour and show their reasoning. Ask students who finish quickly to find 3/4 of 2, 5, and 10 hours or 3/4 of a 20-minute period.

If students are having difficulty, ask:

- How does thinking about the fractions 1/2 and 1/4 help?
- What do you think the fraction 3/4 indicates?
- How could you set this up on a number line?

Make sure that students share at least two solution methods. It is not necessary to share all six.

Heads Up!

Doing the activity may prompt the discovery of other strategies. These can be shared during the review or summary discussion.

List the steps for strategies that work. For example, find 1/4, add 1/4 + 1/4 + 1/4 = 3/4; or add 15/60 + 15/60 + 15/60 = 45/60 = 3/4; or 4/4 (whole) − 1/4 = 3/4 (60/60 − 15/60 = 45/60).

Do one more example as a group.

I have a 12-pack of soda. I intend to give away three-fourths of the pack. How many cans will be left?

What fraction of the pack does that represent?

Students will either find 3/4 of 12 and subtract, or they will grasp the concept of the whole as 4/4, which leaves 1/4 if 3/4 is removed. They then find only 1/4 of 12.

Record students' methods on the board. Use pictures to support the recorded ideas. For example:

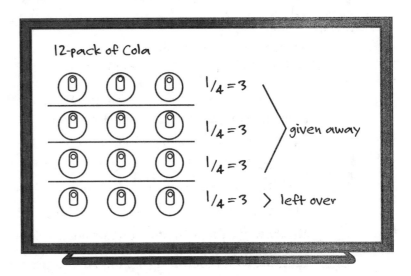

Find one-quarter; then add it up three times and subtract that from the whole.

1/4 + 1/4 + 1/4 = 3/4

3 + 3 + 3 = 9, or 3/12 + 3/12 + 3/12 = 9/12

4/4 − 3/4 = 1/4

12 − 9 = 3

To summarize:

4/4 = 12/12 = the whole

3/4 = 9/12 = part given away/whole

1/4 = 3/12 = part remaining/whole

Show three-fourths on the number line as the complement to one-fourth.

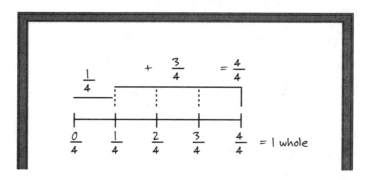

Heads Up!

One issue may need further discussion. The numerator in the answer is not "1," and therefore the process for finding the amount left over requires two steps: first, finding the number in the group when the total is divided by four, and second, determining the total for three of those groups or subtracting one of the groups from the total.

The concept "out of a total" may aid your students. Three-fourths is three out of every four, whereas one-fourth is one out of every four. Students can divide 12 sodas into four groups and count the total number of cans in three groups, or count three out of four cans from each group.

Remind students that they may also hear "three-quarters" as a synonym for three-fourths. If students do not bring it up, introduce the percent equivalent, 75%. Post: "1/2 = 50%, 1/4 = 25%, and 3/4 = 75%."

Activity 1: Seats for 3/4

Introduce the premise and instructions, *Seats for 3/4* (*Student Book*, p. 44).

Money is tight for new buildings. Some schools or factories are considering building cafeterias with a capacity for seating only three-fourths of the workers or students. For each building, determine how many people the cafeteria will seat.

Assign one building to each pair or group of students. Finding three-fourths of 100 may be the easiest problem, but emphasize that for every case students need to show their reasoning with a picture or number line.

Process the problems with questions such as:

How many people could sit in the cafeteria of Building A (or B or C)? How do you know?

What fraction of the total number of people is that? How do you know?

What are the fractions that represent the whole number of workers in the building and the part of that number who *cannot* sit in the cafeteria when it is full?

Summarize and record the strategies used and demonstrated. If no one divides by four and multiplies by three to solve the problem, introduce this strategy and provide another example to which students can apply it (e.g., a building with 80 workers).

Share a number line and a grid example for each building. How are they alike? How are they different? Emphasize making a whole by combining the two groups; the 3/4 who fit in the cafeteria and the 1/4 who do not together equal the 4/4 of all the workers.

Heads Up!

Students need to partition part of the grid to represent each building. Tell them they do not need the whole grid.

Activity 2: Where Are You From?

Refer to p. 46. Explain that the goal is to compare amounts (numbers of people from different countries) to three-fourths of the total number of people polled. Review the directions to make sure everyone understands the task and is working with a partner.

As student pairs work, observe their approaches. Although the problems are presented in number form, encourage students to draw pictures or number lines to find and check their answers.

When students finish, call the group together to share solutions and strategies. As needed, prompt with questions such as the following:

What is the whole? How many are in the whole?

What is the part we are looking at in this problem? How many are in the part? How can we write that as a fraction?

What are some different ways we can tell whether that fraction is more or less than three-fourths?

Summary Discussion

Begin summarizing by asking students:

What is a rule for finding three-fourths?

Will this work for finding three-fourths of any number?

Benchmarks

Discuss which approach students could take to solve a problem with unwieldy numbers. For example, the Web site http://www.ananova.com/2004 reports that dogs "share 75% of human genes." A total of 18,473 of the known 24,567 human genes have a canine version. Is the percent reported by the Web site correct? Try the problem with calculators. Relate the numbers and percentages to fractions. Then ask:

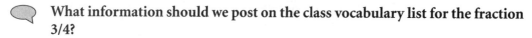 **What information should we post on the class vocabulary list for the fraction 3/4?**

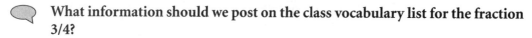 **What does the "4" remind us to do? What does the "3" remind us to do?**

Share ideas and then allow a few moments for students to take notes in *Reflections* (*Student Book*, p. 105).

Practice

Show Me 3/4!, p. 48
For practice finding three-fourths visually.

3/4 Measurements, p. 50

Where to Place It?, p. 52
For practice placing fractions on a number line.

More "How Many, How Far?" Problems, p. 53
For practice solving problems and supporting answers with diagrams.

Missing Quantities—Parts and Wholes, p. 55
For practice finding 1/4, 3/4, or 4/4 when one of those quantities is known.

Extension

3/4 of a Million?, p. 56

Test Practice

Test Practice, p. 57

Looking Closely

Observe whether students are able to

Solve problems by finding three-fourths of a quantity using at least two methods

Note who loses track of the steps and their meanings before arriving at the solution. Reminding these students that three-fourths will be bigger than one-fourth or one-half may be enough to prompt them to check the size of their answers and to correct their own mistakes.

Help students understand the relationship between one-fourth and three-fourths—that three-fourths is three one-fourths and that three-fourths is the part of the whole remaining after one-fourth is removed. This is best done visually.

Relate finding three-fourths to division and multiplication

Three-fourths should be a signal to students that some amount is designated the whole and will be divided into four groups; three-fourths comprises three of the four groups. Even if students choose to divide by "dealing" or to add up instead of multiplying, show them their steps can be written with division and multiplication notation.

Example:

"You made four piles; that is the same as dividing by four.	$12 \div 4$
You found that there were three in each pile.	$12 \div 4 = 3$
So you added up three of the piles.	$3 + 3 + 3$
Each pile represents 1/4, so you know 3/4 of 12 equals nine.	$3 \times 3 = 9$
So finding 3/4 involves both division and multiplication."	

WHAT TO LOOK FOR IN *LESSON 3*	WHO STANDS OUT? (LIST STUDENTS' INITIALS)			NOTES FOR NEXT STEPS
	STRONG	ADEQUATE	NEEDS WORK	
Concept Development • Shows three-fourths • Compares fractions to three-fourths • Connects three-fourths to one-fourth • Relates multiplication and division to finding three-fourths of a quantity				
Expressive Capacity • Uses at least two methods for finding three-fourths • Composes realistic true/false statements from given data				
Use of Tools • Uses arrays to find and/or show three-fourths • Uses diagrams to find and/or show three-fourths • Uses number lines to find and/or show three-fourths				
Notation Use • Uses 3/4 and 75%				

Rationale

The difficulty of working with fractions increases when the numerator is larger than one. Spending time becoming accustomed to the notion of forming fourths (dividing by four) and taking three of those fourths (multiplying by three) is worthwhile as it will allow students to make sense of other fractional amounts with numerators other than one.

Facilitation

The lesson offers opportunities to notate the strategies demonstrated and reported. See *Looking Closely*, p. 44, for one example of how this can be done. Share grid samples and number lines at the end of *Activity 2*. If this is difficult to achieve as a whole class, consider grouping Building A, B, and C representatives together to talk about their graphic representations.

Making the Lesson Easier

Use smaller numbers and numbers readily divisible by four.

Making the Lesson Harder

If students find the problems too easy, change the numbers to two-digit numbers not divisible by four. Suggest students work on *Extension: 3/4 of a Million?* (*Student Book*, p. 56).

Multiple solutions naturally arise when considering the activity problems. Students in one class helped each other develop solutions as they pooled their knowledge. The teacher observed and intervened to help clarify and share strategies for determining three-fourths of the 32 people seated in the cafeteria. She also asked May to explain why her two solutions both worked for finding the answer.

Evelyn counted the people from Asia, Africa, Central America, and the United States and came up with a total of 32 people; but then she couldn't remember how to solve the question of whether the people from Asia (7) and Central America (13) equaled 3/4 of the total number of people or were more or less than 3/4. Her partner, Vivian, reasoned the problem out for her.

Vivian decided to first find fourths, so she made four groups of eight people. "Half is 16," she said and then added that "half of 16 is eight." She wrote down: "16/32 = 1/2 and 8/32 = 1/4." "One-half plus 1/4 equals 24," she explained, "and because 20 is less than 24, it's less than 3/4."

May, who had been working independently, wrote the following for her solution:

$$32 \div 4 = 8 = 1/4 \qquad 3 \times 8 = 24$$

$$32 \times 3 = 96 \qquad 96 \div 4 = 24$$

The teacher, Marilyn, observed some students determining solutions, while others seemed lost. She intervened to ask, "If 8 = 1/4, then how do you find 3/4?" Vivian answered, "Multiply eight by three." Marilyn drew a number line on the board to illustrate this example. When everyone had taken in the example, she added that 32 − 8 (or 1/4 of the people) = 24 (or 3/4 left over).

Marilyn Moses, observed by Marilyn Matzko
Brockton Adult Learning Center, Brockton, MA

Fraction Stations

> *What benchmark fraction comes to mind?*

Synopsis

This lesson provides an opportunity to assess student fluency and flexibility with benchmark fractions. In past lessons, students worked with benchmark fractions to describe small amounts of a total amount of money or time or a number of people; now they will estimate the size of fractions and locate them in the range *between* benchmark fractions.

1. The whole group estimates and then measures the distance from one given point to another to find the benchmark fraction closest to that distance.

2. In pairs, students visit various Fraction Stations.

3. Pairs examine situations, write a fraction for each to describe the amount relative to the whole, and determine that amount relative to the fraction ranges: less than 1/4; between 1/4 and 1/2; between 1/2 and 3/4; or more than 3/4.

4. The class reviews answers and solution methods for the stations, and you summarize strategies used. Students write in *Reflections* (*Student Book*, p. 105) and assess their progress.

Objective

• Compare fractions involving numbers up to 1,000 to determine where they are located in relation to the benchmarks 1/4, 1/2, and 3/4

Materials/Prep

- Blank paper
- Colored markers
- Extra pencils and pens for each station
- Graph paper
- Magnet
- Newsprint or transparencies
- Post-it™ Notes
- Safety pin
- Tape measures or rulers

Mark the door with a small Post-it Note for reference during the *Opening Discussion*. Do *not* place the mark at exactly 1/4, 1/2, or 3/4 of the distance from any of the door's edges.

Prepare and number Fraction Stations ahead of time. Instructions follow.

Station 1: Record data from your class on newsprint. List two categories, for example, gender (male or female) or country of origin (U.S.- or foreign-born). Also write down the total number of class members.

Example:

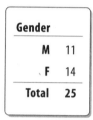

Gender	
M	11
F	14
Total	25

Station 2: Record on newsprint data from a larger group (such as your school program or local neighborhood), for example, number of people on welfare, number who smoke, or number of senior citizens. Record the total population of which your group is a subset, using numbers up to 1,000. (Statistics are available by calling your local Council on Aging or consulting a local reference librarian or a census Web site for your state.)

Station 3: Place on a table a sketchbook, novel, or phonebook with a bookmark inserted in it. Write the total number of pages in the book (should be in the 100's) on a Post-it Note, and stick it on the book's cover.

Station 4: Place a deck of cards on a table.

Station 5: Place on a table a pair of pants or a long-sleeved article of clothing marked with a safety pin that can be described as being "about halfway up" or "a quarter of the way up" from the bottom. Supply tape measures or rulers.

Station 6: Partially fill a cylindrical container with water. Supply tape measures or rulers.

As you set up the stations, make sure the situations cover the whole range of fraction options.

Opening Discussion

Begin the lesson by describing a location using fractions or by staging a situation in which you direct a student to the location of a book. For example, ask:

 Have you ever tried to give directions by saying, for example, "the convenience store is about halfway down the block"? or "Can you get the book that is on the shelf halfway in from the left?"

Students have seen the use of fractions to describe distance in *Lessons 1–3*, but if they are not familiar with taking measurements, model the process, using the example of a mark on a door.

Heads Up!

Emphasize starting at zero or the edge of the ruler. Students unfamiliar with taking measurements might incorrectly place the ruler at the one-inch mark.

Ask students to describe the distance to the mark.

 How could you use fractions to explain the location of the mark from the left edge across the width of the door?

You are looking for answers such as "It's about halfway" or "It is about three-quarters of the way from the left-side edge."

After students have described the placement of the mark from the left and right sides, top, and bottom of the door, measure the total length of the door and the distance to the mark from each location with a measuring tape. *Keep the numbers in round centimeters or inches.* Then confirm students' estimates by writing a fraction to represent the total length and width of the door and the distance to the mark from each door edge (for example, 30"/72"). One at a time, compare these fractions to the benchmarks 1/4, 1/2, and 3/4, using the following phrases:

- Less than 1/4
- Equal to 1/4
- Between 1/4 and 1/2
- Equal to 1/2
- Between 1/2 and 3/4
- Equal to 3/4
- More than 3/4

Ask:

 How is finding a fraction to describe the distance from a door edge to the mark similar to what you have done before with fractions?

If nobody mentions the whole (length or width of the door) and the part (distance to the mark from either the top, bottom, or left or right side), ask:

 What was the part? What was the whole?

Activity: Fraction Stations

Start out by orienting students to the activity.

💬 **Today you will be looking at data, objects, and some measurement situations at different stations. You will write a fraction that describes the situation, choose the benchmark fraction closest to it, and identify where it falls in a *range* between benchmark fractions. You will illustrate that range with a picture, number line, or grid.**

💬 **As you work at each station, use what you have learned in class to make sensible estimates and to check your work mathematically.**

Assign pairs of students the odd- or even-numbered stations.

The language can be overwhelming to students. Take a moment to preview the phrases they will see: "less than 1/4," "equal to 1/4," "between 1/4 and 1/2," "equal to 1/2," "between 1/2 and 3/4," "equal to 3/4," and "greater than 3/4." Use a number line marked from 0 to 12 to demonstrate these fractional amounts.

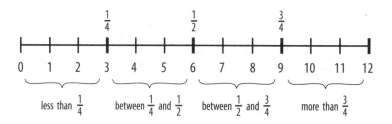

As students work their way through the stations, they record their fractions and reasoning on pp. 60–62, *Student Book*.

Heads Up!

If you want students to work at all six stations, you will need to provide more copies of the *Fraction Stations* worksheets.

Outlined next are the first steps students take at each station. After the first steps, they continue by completing the forms in their books.

Station 1: Data about the Class

Students look at data from the class and write a fraction *describing* something about the data. Then they make statements comparing the size of one category of the data to fraction benchmarks.

Station 2: Statistics about This Neighborhood

Students look at data about the class's neighborhood/region/area and write fractions *describing* the local data in terms of the whole data set. Then they locate their function on a number line and use a benchmark fraction to describe the data.

Station 3: Cut the Deck

Students estimate the number of cards in one pile compared to the whole deck of cards (52).

Each pair cuts the deck and, using benchmarks, *estimates* the size of both piles relative to the whole deck. They write their estimated fractions and then check their estimates by counting. They record both the estimated and the actual fractions.

Station 4: A Bookmarked Page

Students estimate the fraction of the book "read" (indicated by the placement of the bookmark) and then open the book to check their estimates against the actual page number. They record both the estimated and the actual fractions.

Station 5: Pinned Piece of Clothing

Students estimate and describe with a fraction the location of a safety pin relative to the bottom edge of a sleeve or pant leg.

Each student measures (with tape measure or ruler) the distance from the pin to the edge and the length of the sleeve or pant leg to calculate a more exact fraction. They record estimates and actual fractions.

Station 6: How Full Is the Container?

Students describe how full a container is. They might use a ruler or a calibrated measuring cup to verify their estimates.

Allow 20–30 minutes for students to work at the stations before gathering the class for the *Summary Discussion*.

Notice which fraction equivalents appear to be easy or hard for students to calculate when they are establishing ranges. Be prepared to summarize strategies students use during the exercise—dividing by the denominator; finding a half of a half; dividing and then multiplying; finding one-fourth and subtracting from the whole; and so on.

Stations Review

Draw the class together to review the *Fraction Stations* problems and answers, especially those that seemed hard.

Next review the answers and discuss fully at least one of each station type (either 1 or 2; 3 or 4; and 5 or 6).

Ask:

What helped you figure out the benchmark fraction you chose?

What was important to know at this station?

Summarize and record for students the strategies you saw and heard used during the exercise.

Summary Discussion

Benchmarks

Explain to the class that the next two lessons will focus on the benchmark 1/10.

 Before we move on to one-tenth, we will review again some of the strategies we used to find one-half, one-fourth, and three-fourths of any amount.

As students share strategies, focus on those that can be notated, and include verbal and physical explanations with notation.

Ask some general questions to help students as they continue to study decimals and percents:

 How are 0/2 and 0/4 alike? How are they different?

 How are 2/2 and 4/4 alike? How are they different?

Remind students to record their thoughts about their progress in *Reflections* (*Student Book*, p. 105). It will be useful for you to read these reflection pieces because they ask students to self-assess their progress.

Practice

Less Than, More Than, Equal to, or Between?, p. 63
For practice determining where a measurement falls in relation to one the benchmarks.

Extension

Describing Data, p. 65
For practice describing data using fraction intervals.

Fractions of Billions, p. 68
For challenging work with large numbers.

Test Practice

Test Practice, p. 69

Looking Closely

Compare fractions involving numbers up to 1,000 to determine where they are located in relation to the benchmarks 1/4, 1/2, and 3/4

Do students quickly recognize amounts close to the benchmark fractions 1/4, 1/2, and 3/4? As they work at the different stations, note whether they are able to set up a fraction and estimate its size relative to the benchmarks. If they have difficulty, suggest they begin by drawing a diagram, number line, or grid representation. Number lines are particularly effective tools for locating the fractions.

If students have located a fraction close to a benchmark fraction, identifying whether it is more or less than the benchmark should follow. However, even if they are able to say that a fraction is more than 1/2, they may not be able to establish whether it is also less than 3/4. Probe for that understanding.

Encourage students to check their work by using a different strategy and sharing with others who approached the problem in a different way.

WHAT TO LOOK FOR IN *LESSON 4*	WHO STANDS OUT? (LIST STUDENTS' INITIALS)			NOTES FOR NEXT STEPS
	STRONG	ADEQUATE	NEEDS WORK	
Concept Development • Recognizes fractions equivalent to one-half • Recognizes fractions equivalent to one-quarter • Recognizes fractions equivalent to three-quarters • Places part-whole amounts in the correct location with respect to the benchmark fractions • Determines range of fractions (between 1/4 and 1/2, etc.)				
Expressive Capacity • Uses "out of" or "part-whole" or "groups" to explain the set-up of a fraction				
Use of Tools • Measures accurately • Uses number line or grid				
Notation Use • Uses part-whole relationships appropriately when writing fractions				

Rationale

Locating fractions *between* benchmarks sharpens students' fraction skills, as it strengthens understanding of the relative sizes of benchmark fractions. By addressing a variety of situations in which comparative descriptions are required, students become more proficient and precise when communicating mathematically.

Math Background

To locate a fraction requires knowing how to find equivalents for each of the benchmark fractions, thus establishing the parameters for the problem. Students might complete the calculations in any order; however, starting by finding one-half is the easiest, most efficient process. From there, they can determine whether the fraction is larger or smaller than one-half so they know which benchmark (one-fourth or three-fourths) to look at next.

Fractions such as 11/25 can easily be compared to benchmark fractions using the part-whole model. In this case, the whole is 25. Half of 25 is 12 1/2. The part, 11, is less than 12 1/2, so the fraction, 11/25, is less than 1/2. This is the kind of reasoning that students have been encouraged to use throughout this unit, giving them repeated opportunities to practice mental math (halving, doubling, quartering, and multiplying by three).

Facilitation

If students leave their answers at the stations on Post-it Notes, folded or otherwise hidden, the last group at a station could be in charge of evaluating all the answers.

Making the Lesson Easier

Choose a book with an even number of pages so that determining the location of the bookmark is easier. Likewise, simplify the location of the safety pin.

Making the Lesson Harder

Add a station with statistics about the United States. Encourage students to work with unwieldy numbers by rounding and with large numbers by decomposing.

Add a station at which students compare the distance from their classroom to City A vs. from their classroom to City B, using the benchmark fractions (less than 1/4; between 1/4 and 1/2; between 1/2 and 3/4; or more than 3/4).

Even students with good number sense find picking the right range a challenge.

One student was at the station with the bookmark in the book.

Student: "It's less than 1/2. I know that."

Observer: "How do you know?"

Student: "Three hundred and twenty-two is less than 1/2 because 322 + 322 is 644."

Observer: "There are 760 pages total, so what would half be?"

The student did not seem entirely sure. He tried the number 380. We checked on the calculator; he was right.

Observer: "And one-fourth?"

Student: "One hundred and sixty-five?"

This student was clearly more comfortable adding up than he was dividing. He was good at adding too. When he saw the answer was 190, he said, "I should have known that." Then he said 322 was less than one-fourth.

Observer: "How do you know that?"

Student: "It is not half, but it's close to it."

This student was not alone. A few members of the group were having trouble picking the right range. Choosing a range may be a more complex task than picking out the closest benchmark fraction, as one teacher theorized.

It was not this student's inclination to do a number line or make a table, but without some way to organize the numbers, his written work did not reflect his strong estimation skills or his ability to check his work with mental math.

Later he asked me, "Do you always have to do a number line?" When he did one for a different problem, I saw that he drew every mark on the line from 0 to 32. Together we drew a few other versions of number lines so he could see that every number does not have to be indicated on the line.

Susanne Campagna, observed by Martha Merson
Read, Write, Now, Springfield, MA

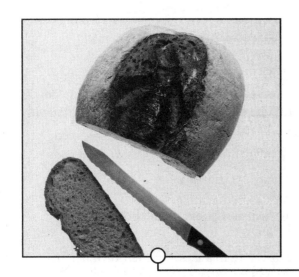

One-Tenth

> *How can you cut a loaf into tenths?*

Synopsis

In this lesson, students begin to explore the benchmark fraction 1/10 as they visit five stations. Later they numerically describe one-tenth, including the decimal 0.1. Students brainstorm everyday names for one-tenth in preparation for the work on decimals in the next lesson.

1. Students brainstorm ways to find one-tenth of a given amount.

2. Student pairs visit stations in which they find one-tenth of different amounts and objects.

3. Student pairs share how they found one-tenth at the different stations and discuss how they knew it was one-tenth.

4. The whole class writes one-tenth in various ways.

Objectives

- Find one-tenth of a quantity
- Identify multiple representations for one-tenth, such as 1/10, 0.1, .1, 10%, and visual models

Materials/Prep

Set up five stations. Make duplicate stations if you have a large class. Details about station set up and what happens are as follows:

Station 1: Paper Clips

- One box of 100 paper clips
- 100 pennies and 10 dimes (optional)

Students answer the questions: "What is a tenth of the whole box? How do you know?" They record their answers with their explanations on p. 72 in the *Student Book*.

Station 2: Your Height

- Measuring tapes (in inches)
- Various objects around the room, such as a book, a chalkboard eraser, pencils, chalk, a glass or cup, etc.

Students find objects in the room that are close to a tenth of their own heights. They explain their choice and reasoning in their *Student Books*.

Station 3: Index Card

- 3" x 5" index cards
- Ruler
- Scissors
- Scotch tape

Each student cuts one-tenth out of an index card and tapes the tenth in his or her *Student Book*. When the class shares results, you will pick a few of the tenths they cut to discuss whether they do indeed all equal one-tenth.

Station 4: One Quarter

- One quarter (25¢)
- 25 pennies for reference

Students find one-tenth of a quarter and explain how they know their answer is correct.

Station 5: Stamp Collection

- 4 stamps or copy and cut *Blackline Master 1*

Students solve the following problem: "The stamps at the station represent one-tenth of someone's collection. How many stamps are in the whole collection?" They write their answers and how they arrived at them in their *Student Books*.

Opening Discussion

Begin by saying:

 In some communities, people voluntarily contribute a *tithe* for the support of their church. What is a tithe?

If nobody can define it, explain that a tithe is a voluntary donation of **one-tenth** of a person's income. Then add:

 My cousin Lisa can barely make ends meet, even by working two jobs. She makes $600 a week. She is worried that the tithe will be a lot. What do you think? How much will she need to contribute in her tithe?

Ask students to think about the problem and share their thoughts with a neighbor. When all are ready, have the class share. Ask:

 How did you find the tithe based on Lisa's salary?

Heads Up!

This is an introduction to thinking about one-tenth. Most students will likely come up with $60. Probe for why. Do not go into long explanations about how to find a tenth. Listen to students' reasoning and take notes on the board. For example, "One-tenth of 100 is 10, so 1/10 of 600 is 6 × 10, or 60."

Tell students that they will find a tenth of various amounts as they go through the five stations.

Activity 1: Show Me 1/10! Stations

Pairs of students visit each station to show one-tenth of various things or amounts as they answer the questions, write their explanations, and make drawings in their *Student Books*.

Station 1: Paper Clips

Students look at a total of 100 paper clips and either know that 1/10 is 10 paper clips, divide 100 by 10 to find the answer, or make 10 groups to find the number in one group. In all cases, students are working with a *discrete model* of the fraction 1/10.

Station 2: Your Height

Each student selects an object in the classroom that is about one-tenth of his or her height. Students estimate the length of their chosen objects. Probe for how they are making their choices. The measuring tapes available at the station are for those students who want to measure their height and/or objects.

Heads Up!

Do this activity yourself before class so you see the different possible cuts.

Students determine one-tenth of the index card, cut it out, and tape their tenths in their *Student Books*. Note that the strip could be horizontal or vertical, and the shapes of the tenths—for example, long and skinny or short and wide—can vary. Make a note of which ones you want them to share with the class later so there is a variety to use in proving that they all represent one-tenth of the index card.

Station 4: One-Quarter

Students determine one-tenth of a quarter. For students who rely on counting or grouping, the pennies at the station will be helpful. The problem of finding a tenth of a number not evenly divisible by 10 makes this a potentially arithmetically challenging station.

Station 5: Stamp Collection

Students are given one-tenth of a stamp collection and must determine the number of stamps in the entire collection. They have visited stations where the whole was given and they had to find the part (one-tenth); at this station, the part is given and they must find the total (the whole).

After pairs visit the stations and solve the problems, gather the whole class together. Tell them:

> **You have worked with one-tenth in a variety of ways. What surprised you?**

Students share a few of their surprises and then review the problems at the stations. Start with the problem that involves finding one-tenth of the paper clips, and quickly establish the correct answer as "10." Move to Station 2 and examine some students' heights and the objects they chose to represent one-tenth of those heights. Ask:

> **How do you know this object is about one-tenth of your height?**

For Station 3, gather some strips that students cut in different ways, and post them for all to see. Ask:

> **These strips look quite different. How could we show that these are all one-tenth of the index card?**

Students might need to cut some of their tenths to "fit" them into another one, as in the following example:

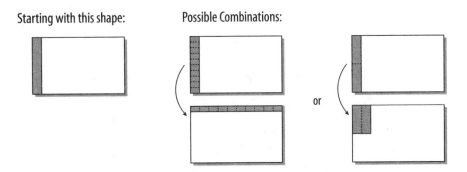

Starting with this shape:

Possible Combinations:

or

When students share their solutions for finding one-tenth of a quarter (2.5¢), probe by asking:

How do you know you have the correct answer?

Finally, Station 5 poses a different dilemma for students: They have found one-tenth of different things and/or amounts. Now they are given one-tenth of a stamp collection and asked to find the total stamps in the collection. If students find it helpful to group, they might draw ten groups, each with four stamps, to find the total. Explore their solutions further by again asking:

How do you know your answer is correct?

Activity 2: Ways to Represent One-Tenth

Write the words "one-tenth" on the blackboard. Invite students to write responses on the board as you ask:

What is another way to write one-tenth? Who has another way?

How would your read each of these numbers?

Post the term "one-tenth" and its representations on the class vocabulary list. If all of the following notation are not mentioned, you add the missing ones:

- 1/10
- 0.1
- .1
- 10%

Note: This is an ideal time to emphasize the "-th" ending as a signifier for fractions, as in one-fourth, one-fifth, and one-tenth. Some students are familiar with 10% as the equivalent to 1/10. Probe to clarify the connection between 10% and 1/10.

Summary Discussion

Review the ways to say, write, and describe one-tenth by posting the following chart on the board or on a large piece of newsprint.

Benchmarks

Number	1/10	.1	0.1
Word Description			

Encourage the inclusion of several word descriptions for each column and a different graphic for each of the tenth numbers (number lines, grids, diagrams, etc.)

Articulate observations about zeros, including trailing zeros and zeros as important and unimportant placeholders (for example, 0.1 versus .01).

Ask:

 What makes one-tenth a benchmark fraction or *decimal?*

Brainstorm some ideas about how tenths are used to mark miles on an odometer in a car, measure medicine prescriptions, report test scores, and mark time in sports events, to name a few. Also, if no one else mentions it, raise the idea of tenths being a natural extension of our base ten number system (see *Lesson Commentary*, p. 67, for more on this).

On the class vocabulary list, add the term "one-tenth." Close by inviting students to write about one-tenth, what it means to them, and how they find one-tenth of a quantity in *Reflections* (*Student Book*, p. 106).

Practice

I Will Show You 1/10!, p. 76
For practice finding one-tenth.

Containers, p. 77
For practice marking one-tenth.

More or Less?, p. 78
For practice determining more or less than one-tenth.

Extension

More Tenths, p. 79
For using tenths to talk about halves and quarters.

EMPower™

Test Practice

Test Practice, p. 80.

 ## Looking Closely

Observe whether students are able to

Find one-tenth of a quantity

Are students able to find one-tenth of different quantities? Note whether students have a way of finding one-tenth that they use consistently, change their strategy given the situation, or start anew with each problem. For example, they might make ten groups, sort objects into ten piles, divide by ten, move the decimal point, or count by ones. In each case, make sure they are able to explain how they know they have determined one-tenth of an amount.

In Station 5, where students are given one-tenth and asked to find the whole, observe their strategies. If they have a hard time with the problem, remind them to think about how they found one-tenth of the paper clips.

Identify multiple representations for one-tenth, such as 1/10, 0.1, .1, 10%, and visual models

Are students able to represent one-tenth in a variety of ways? Note everyday references they use when talking about one-tenth.

WHAT TO LOOK FOR IN *LESSON 5*	WHO STANDS OUT? (LIST STUDENTS' INITIALS)			NOTES FOR NEXT STEPS
	STRONG	ADEQUATE	NEEDS WORK	
Concept Development • Shows one-tenth when finding one-tenth of various quantities				
Expressive Capacity • Uses "tenths" to describe fractions • Uses decimals (0.1 or .1) to describe tenths				
Use of Tools • Uses a measuring tape to show how an object is one-tenth of his or her height • Uses a ruler to find the length or width of an index card to determine one-tenth of the card				
Notation Use • Uses numerals to notate one-tenth in various ways including 1/10, 0.1, 0.1, and 10%				

Rationale

Students' repertoire of benchmarks is expanded to include one-tenth, an often used fraction, decimal, and percent. People find it easy to work with 10 and its multiples and factors. Although finding one-tenth has long been taught as "moving the decimal," in this unit, students focus on understanding one-tenth by physically, pictorially, and numerically finding one-tenth of various quantities. By relying on developing an understanding of tenths, the all-too-common misuses of memorized facts are avoided.

Math Background

In the United States we use the English Standard system of measurement—inches, feet, and yards. However, there has long been a movement toward converting to the metric system based on the number 10. Widely used around the world, the metric system makes it easy to compute. Regardless of the standard of measurement used, one-tenth is a benchmark fraction, decimal, and percent. In everyday life, our monetary system is based on 10; for example, one dollar has 10 dimes and 100 pennies. Decimals are used extensively to describe measurements, time, and money (e.g., 1.2 million dollars). Percents, also based on 10, are widely used to describe information (e.g., 10% increase, 6% tax, 55% of voters, etc.).

Finding one-tenth of 10, 20, 30, 40, or any multiple of 10 is relatively simple. When those amounts are larger—say 200, 300, or 400—students are not always sure whether the tenth is 2 or 20, 3 or 30, or 4 or 40. The activities in this lesson establish clarity on this issue, and students can move on to finding one-tenth of numbers that are not multiples of 10, for example, 25. By using manipulatives, students who cannot figure out the problem mathematically are able to arrive at the solution. Alternatively, given a number or quantity that represents one-tenth of a total, how can the total be found? This problem forces students to break the whole to make 10 parts and—in the case of finding the whole—put the parts together again to make the whole. Students will have worked with these same ideas with whole numbers in the *Everyday Numbers* unit, and they now extend these concepts to fractions, decimals, and percents.

Facilitation

Most of this lesson is focused on reviewing the findings at the stations students visit, with the emphasis on finding a tenth and representing it in various ways. The stations provide situations that help students understand and problem-solve ideas about tenths. Do not push for formulas, rules, or tricks you know. If students bring them up, ask for an explanation of their meanings and how they work.

Making the Lesson Easier

If you see that students are struggling at any particular station, encourage them to use pennies, paper clips, or any other easy-to-count objects to make sense of the problem. Then if you see them struggling again at another station, ask them how what they learned when they used the manipulatives could help them in this new situation.

Making the Lesson Harder

If the numbers at the stations are too easy for some students, use less "friendly" numbers, but only after you have ascertained that these students have a true visual understanding. Ask students to use a picture or drawing to show their reasoning and to make up a problem involving tenths for others to solve after first solving it themselves with a picture.

6

More About One-Tenth

Where is the tenth?

Synopsis

In this lesson, students continue working with the decimal form of one-tenth (0.1) and with the percent form (10%) to understand their relationship to the fraction 1/10.

1. Students match each others' cards displaying different quantities, and then the class examines matches for one-tenth.

2. Students use various representations of 1/10 and 9/10 to illustrate different situations.

3. Students focus on how 10% is 1/10.

4. The whole class reviews names of and descriptions for one-tenth.

Objectives

- Work with multiple representations equivalent to one-tenth
- Use 1/10 and 9/10 in different contexts

Materials/Prep

Copy and cut *Match Cards* (*Blackline Master 2*). Make sufficient copies so that each student receives at least one card for *Activity 1*, and at the close of *Activity 1*, each student receives a complete copy of *Match Cards*.

Opening Discussion

Review quickly the *Summary Discussion* at the end of *Lesson 5*. Say:

We said there were many ways to represent one-tenth. Remind me of some of them.

As students share, make sure that all the fraction, decimal, and percent names for one-tenth are listed. They will need to recognize them in *Activity 1, One-Tenth Match*.

Activity 1: One-Tenth Match

Distribute to each student one or more cards from the *Match Cards* (*Blackline Master 2*). Instruct students to mingle until they find their card's match in words or numbers. Note that there are multiple matches for some of the cards, but they need only find one card to match each of theirs at this point.

Every pair of students posts their matching cards. Students then review the pairings and on p. 82 of the *Student Book*, they list all the cards they think represent one-tenth.

Ask students:

If you have a card that shows one-tenth, stand by your card. Does everyone agree that all these cards are equivalent? Why or why not?

Post all the one-tenth cards together, and distribute copies of the *Match Cards* (*Blackline Master 2*) so students can check off the matches equal to one-tenth.

Are there any cards that show one-tenth but are not checked off?

Invite students to share their ideas and images for one-tenth. Lay the groundwork for using one-tenth as a benchmark for comparison.

When you think about one-tenth, do you picture it in one of these ways? If not, how do you picture it?

Of the cards that are left, how would you organize them from smallest amount to largest? Why?

How does one-tenth compare with the benchmark fractions? (Smaller than 3/4, 1/2, and 1/4)

Activity 2: One-Tenth, Nine-Tenths

Looking at 9/10 as the complement of 1/10 is important for understanding the whole. In this activity, students will illustrate both of these fractions (or decimals or percents) in a variety of ways.

Refer students to *Activity 2* (*Student Book*, p. 83), and do the first example with them. These common sayings reflect the use of one-tenth and nine-tenths in everyday life. Two ways of expressing the same thing are given for each saying. Elicit from students a way to represent the two fractions in the example, using a grid, a line, or a circle. Then have them do the rest of the sayings on their own or in pairs.

When students are done, ask:

 What did you notice in all the sayings about one-tenth and nine-tenths?

What was the same? What was different?

In the next activity, students will focus on the relation between the fraction 1/10 and the percent form, 10%.

Activity 3: Why Is 10% Equal to 1/10?

Refer students to *Activity 3* (*Student Book*, p. 85), allowing time for each person to show why 10% equals 1/10. This activity reinforces students' understanding of the fact that the "10" in 10% is not related to the "10" in 1/10. Ten out of 100 (10%) should be connected to the concept of "1 out of 10," or 1/10.

Summary Discussion

Review the ways to say, write, and describe one-tenth by posting the following chart on the board or on a large piece of newsprint.

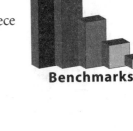

Benchmarks

Number	1/10	.1	0.1
Word Description			
Graphic			

Encourage the inclusion of several word descriptions for each column and a different graphic for each of the tenth numbers (number lines, grids, diagrams, etc.).

Articulate observations about zeros, including trailing zeros and zeros as important and unimportant placeholders (for example 0.1, versus .01).

Ask:

 One-tenth is a benchmark fraction, decimal, and percent. Where do you see one-tenth (1/10, 0.1, .1, and 10%) used in your daily life?

On the class vocabulary list, add the terms "0.1 and .1," and revisit the working definition for "**decimal point.**" Close by inviting students to write about what 0.1 means to them and how they find 0.1 of a quantity in *Reflections* (*Student Book*, p. 107).

Practice

Make a Gauge, p. 86
For practice marking increments of one-tenth and labeling them as decimals.

Location, Location, Location, p. 87
For practice locating decimals on a number line-like map and adding decimals.

Gaining Weight, p. 88
For practice finding 0.1 of a quantity.

Grid Visions, p. 89
For practice finding 0.1 of related amounts.

 Extension

Reimbursement Changes, p. 91
For practice finding 0.1 and 1/4 of different dollar amounts.

 Test Practice

Test Practice, p. 93

Looking Closely

Observe whether students are able to

Identify multiple representations equivalent to one-tenth, such as 1/10, 0.1, .1, 10%, and visual models

Are students able to match up the cards that represent one-tenth in a variety of ways? Check students' work when they review matched cards and list those equal to one-tenth to see whether they are able to identify the various representations of one-tenth. Where there is disagreement, encourage discussion, asking students to prove their points. Ask *how* they know a card is or is not equal to one-tenth.

The conversation about those cards *not* equivalent to one-tenth is also important. Do students recognize the difference between .1 and 1.? "Less than a whole" and "more than a whole" are important ideas, as is the whole, 100%, and the entire shaded grid. Note that although number lines are used here for the first time in this unit, students should recognize them. In this lesson, students will identify numbers marked with arrows on the lines instead of using the number lines to find a part of a whole. If students are not familiar with this process, help them by counting the hash marks.

Use 1/10 and 9/10 in different contexts

Do students have various ways of naming and writing 1/10 and 9/10? The contexts given could help students see the fraction, decimal, and percent equivalents of one-tenth and nine-tenths. They use various representations—a line, a grid, and a circle—to illustrate the two quantities. Students familiar with circle graphs might see 10% and 90% best with such a graph; for others, line graphs will make more sense; and for yet others, grids will be best, especially if they need to count by ones.

Do students notice that 1/10 and 9/10 together make a whole? If they use a circle graph, ask why the two parts cover the whole circle. If the parts do not cover the circle, ask what the leftover part of the circle is. If, instead, students use a number line or a grid, ask them to show you the whole and the parts, and ask why those two parts equal the whole. This is a case where it make sense to use percents, and students will likely mention them.

WHAT TO LOOK FOR IN *LESSON 6*	WHO STANDS OUT? (LIST STUDENTS' INITIALS)			NOTES FOR NEXT STEPS
	STRONG	ADEQUATE	NEEDS WORK	
Concept Development • Identifies 1/10 in multiple represenations • Uses 1/10 and 9/10 in various contexts				
Expressive Capacity • Uses the term "tenths" to describe decimal fractions				
Use of Tools • Demonstrates with grids, number lines, and circles • Connects diagrams, number lines, and grids with appropriate decimal fractions				
Notation Use • Matches decimal, fraction, and percent forms for one-tenth • Recognizes 10% as an equivalent for 1/10 and .1				

Rationale

Tenths are critical to an understanding of money, measurement, percents, and scientific notation. Because decimals look much like whole numbers, students often complete operations with them without solidly understanding their meaning and, therefore, misinterpret solutions. They might multiply 0.2×5 and write "10" rather than "1." Clarifying the fraction-decimal relationship solidifies students' understandings of the decimal values and aids their reasoning about solution values.

Associating the decimal fraction with the common fraction is as much a language issue as a mathematical issue. Help students establish the connection between the two by using the term "one-tenth" to refer to both decimal and common forms of the fraction. Practice is key to forming solid associations.

To reinforce the different notation, make a poster with all the representations for one-tenth. Leave it on the wall so that students can add to it throughout the unit.

Math Background

We use a base 10 number system. Counting to 10, counting by 10's, the fraction one-tenth, the decimal 0.1, and the percent 10% are all part of our everyday usage of number. However, it is also the case that students are often not sufficiently grounded in their understanding of all these forms to be able to manipulate them correctly later when they operate with tenths. One-tenth of a 10-piece candy bar is easy to find; it is not as simple to figure out one-tenth of a 12-piece candy bar. Understanding tenths, then, often involves understanding parts and wholes and the relationship between them.

Historical Background: The Hindu place-value system was in use for nearly 1,000 years before decimal fractions were introduced in the 16th century as a way to notate square roots of irrational numbers. The decimal point was not commonly used to separate whole numbers and decimal fractions until the first half of the 1700's. There is still no universal way to represent decimal fractions. Some people use a comma; some a point, as we do in the U.S.; and some a point as the English do: 53·25. (See *Historical Topics for the Mathematics Classroom*, NCTM, 1989, for more.)

Facilitation

Although the ideas and activities may seem trivial at first glance, our field-test experience tells us that students' conceptions of tenths in their various forms (fractions, decimals, and percents) are not solid. Urge students to demonstrate their understanding, to share it with you and their peers, and to think about the different forms of notation.

Making the Lesson Easier

For students struggling to match the cards, start them with fewer cards and omit those that are greater than one. For students unfamiliar with circle graphs, share how you would illustrate the first example of *Activity 2*, using a circle. Stress that the circle represents the whole and the two parts and, though not precisely accurate, should show 1/10 and 9/10.

Making the Lesson Harder

Connect decimal and whole number place value with scientific notation (powers of 10). The book *Powers of Ten*, by Philip and Phylis Morrison, is an excellent visual and mathematical resource on the subject.

Suggest students do the *Extension* on p. 91.

Facilitating Closing the Unit: Benchmarks Revisited

> *How can you use familiar fractions, decimals, or percents to describe this group?*

Synopsis

This lesson is an opportunity for students to synthesize what they have learned about benchmark fractions, decimals, and percents. Anticipate spending two class sessions if you do all three activities.

1. The whole class describes a crowd using fractions, decimals, percents, and whole numbers.

2. The class reviews the unit by brainstorming all the lessons and skills they remember learning.

3. Students revisit their work from other lessons, and each creates a portfolio of his or her best work.

4. Students complete tasks on the *Final Assessment*.

5. Students complete new Mind Maps and compare their initial and final versions.

Objectives

- Interpret information using fractions, decimals, and percents
- Use the equivalencies for tenths and the whole in fractions, decimals, and percents

Materials/Prep

- Index cards or large Post-it Notes
- Markers
- Newsprint

Copy the *Final Assessment* (*Appendices*, p. 95), one for each student.

Opening Discussion

Review the highlights of the last class, especially the connection between 1/10, 0.1, and 10%. Trigger discussion by posting on the board 100%, .1, 0.1, 1, 1.0, and 20/20, and ask:

 Which of these numbers could you use to describe the portion of the group wearing glasses?

Address any lingering questions, using diagrams, number lines, and grids to support statements.

Tell students that information about decimals and percents, along with everything they have learned in the unit, will be reviewed in this final session.

Activity 1: Standing Up

This activity acts as a class review and general assessment of students' ability to find benchmark fractions and decimals of a given amount, using a number line. It also helps solidify understanding of one-tenth and its complement, nine-tenths.

Distribute markers, index cards, and large Post-it Notes as needed.

Refer to the long, horizontal line on the board (the longer, the better). Tell the class it represents a long line of demonstrators, 800 people total, who participated in a protest march.

 I would like to share some of the *statistics* about that group of marchers. After I share a statistic, I want someone to show the fraction on the number line and write on the board the amount of people represented by that fraction.

Heads Up!

If you decide to use a real-life event, specify a cause for the protest, and change the number to make the story more realistic, note that students might need more time if the numbers are "messy."

Write the italicized portion of the following questions on the board as you ask each question. Ask for volunteers to mark the answers at the right location on the line. See the accompanying graphic for a sense of how this might look on your board.

Half the marchers were adult women. **Who can mark that fraction for the adult women marchers and tell us the number of people it represents?** (Answers: 1/2, 400/800, and the number 400.)

Three-fourths of the marchers were adults. **How many is that? Who can post the fraction and the number of adult marchers?** (Answers: 3/4, 600/800, and the number 600.)

How many were men? **Who can post the number of adult men and the fraction of total marchers they represent?** (Answers: 1/4, 200/800, and the number 200). Note: Suggest students show this fraction as the 1/4 remaining in the adult's 3/4 segment after 1/2 the people are accounted for as adult women.

What fraction were children? (Answers: 1/4, 200/800, and the number 200). *Note:* Suggest students show this fraction as the 1/4 remaining after 3/4 of the people are accounted for as adults.

Ten percent traveled more than 10 miles to the march. **How many is that? Who can post the fraction and the number represented by those who traveled more than 10 miles?** (Answers: 1/10, 80/800, and the number 80).

Nine-tenths of the marchers will be personally affected. **Who can post the fraction and the number for those personally affected?** (Answers: 9/10, 720/800, and the number 720).

All marchers were peaceful. **Who can post the fraction, decimal, and percent figures that stand for all the marchers?** (Answers: 800/800, 1.0, and 100%).

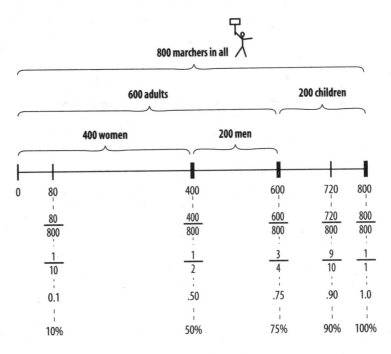

Ask for volunteers to write the matching decimals and percents for all the fractions they have posted that are also benchmarks.

Post your newsprint questions. Students refer to the numbers posted on the line and vote whether each statement is true or false.

- Is it true that 25% is larger than one-tenth?
- Is it true that 90% is larger than three-quarters?
- Is it true that one-tenth more than 800 is 880?

If students have trouble seeing the equivalency between 1.0 and 100%, work with complementary parts, such as 0.1 and 0.9 to show that added together they equal the whole, or 1.0.

If students still have trouble with the equivalencies 1/10, 10%, and 0.1, ask:

How is this situation like the ones in the bar problems you did in the last lesson? How is it different?

What questions do you still have about 1/10, 10%, and 0.1?

Address any misunderstandings by reiterating that the whole in this situation is one whole crowd. Conclude by making sure everyone reaches agreement when you ask:

If the number of marchers were 200, what would 100% be?

How would you write 100% as a decimal?

If a diet chocolate bar contains 30 calories, how many calories would be in 10% of the bar?

How would you write 10% as a decimal? As a fraction?

After students agree on the particulars, ask for different fractions that equal 100%.

✆ Activity 2: Review Session

In this review session, students discuss with a partner answers to your questions about the last activity. Ask:

What skills and knowledge did you use in the last activity that you were not aware of having a few weeks ago?

What was hard for you? What did you feel confident about?

Share a few responses, and then explain that the next activity involves a deeper review of what they have learned in this unit.

Heads Up!

Building in a review session before giving the *Final Assessment* is an opportunity for students to practice study skills.

Tell students:

💬 **One way to prepare for a test is to go over in your mind everything you have learned. We will list all the lessons we have covered so far.**

💬 **What knowledge and skills have you gained?**

After brainstorming, students turn to *Review Session* (*Student Book*, p. 97) and look over the directions before undertaking the activity. When they have finished the lesson review, they start work on their portfolios. Directions are on p. 98 of the *Student Book*.

As students work, suggest practices for them to revisit. If they have not completed practices in some lessons, this is a good time for them to do one or two problems from a practice you suggest.

Collect portfolios as they are completed. Everyone, however, should work on *Activity 3: Final Assessment* at the same time; if some students have not completed their portfolios when most of the class is ready to move on, suggest they complete their portfolios for homework.

⟳ Activity 3: Final Assessment

Remind students that they are to check off the box that best describes how they feel about their ability to solve the task: "Can do," "Don't know how," or "Not sure," and then to complete the task if they can. Tasks do not need to be completed in order; students may choose where they would like to begin.

When students finish, review their responses as a group, and collect all work to assess.

Students work independently on their new Mind Maps. When they have completed them, return their original Mind Maps so they can compare the two.

Summary Discussion

First draw a large "Benchmark Fractions, Decimals, and Percents" Mind Map on the board. Ask students to call out ideas, and connect them to form the class Mind Map. When the map appears full, ask:

Benchmarks

💬 **When you compared your new Mind Maps to your original Mind Maps, what did you notice?**

Next present the play, *Superiority Complex* (*Blackline Master 4*). Ask different students to play the roles of Fractions, Decimals, and Percents. Introduce the play as an imaginary conversation between spokespersons for each of the three types of numbers. When the play ends, ask:

💬 **Which of the three types of representation—fractions, decimals, or percents—is your favorite? Why?**

For closure ask students to complete the sentence, "What I will remember about benchmark fractions, decimals, and percents is . . ."

Assign any unfinished practices that you feel might help students with areas of difficulty.

 ## Looking Closely

Observe whether students are able to

Interpret information using fractions, decimals, and percents

Do students compare part-whole relationships to the benchmark fractions? They should be able to use a visual representation to illustrate their reasoning. When they decide on a benchmark fraction, do they quickly make the connection to equivalent benchmark decimals and/or other percents? Referring to them interchangeably will help students do this. When determining which benchmark fraction, decimal, or percent best approximates a given part-whole, mental math is important. Pay attention to how students make those estimates. For example, "5/11 is close to 1/2 because 5/10 is 1/2" or "because 5 is almost half of 11."

Use the equivalencies for tenths and the whole in fractions, decimals, and percents

Do students understand the different ways to write tenths and one (whole)? If not, revisit degrees on a thermometer as a way to count tenths and arrive at one whole degree. Find 10% and 1/10 of crowds of different sizes. Count 10 tenths to arrive at one whole. Similarly, count, multiply, or add 10's to arrive at 100%. Plan to spend more time on this when students again encounter 10%. The idea of 100% equaling one (whole) may be unfamiliar to your students, and their understanding of it should not be taken for granted.

Rationale

The activity in this lesson provides a chance for you to observe how students integrate and apply what they have learned from past lessons. Students can use each other as resources but should rely on minimal help from you.

Facilitation

The time required for each activity varies, depending on the level of your class. Although it is meant to be an assessment, *Closing the Unit: Benchmarks Revisited* may turn out to be a lesson instead. If this is the case, do no more than one activity per lesson, allowing time for students to return to earlier practices.

Making the Lesson Easier

Change the number of marchers to 40.

Making the Lesson Harder

Change the number of the crowd to 750 or 1,300.

One day a student challenged me to explain "why the numbers got bigger." He was referring to the fact that 0.5 and 50% can both stand for a half, but 50% looks 10 times bigger than the other representation. I wanted to convey that the world of decimals and the world of fractions and percents have different applications and are useful in different ways.

In the next class, we read the play as a jumping-off point for looking at a label from a bottle of water, looking at a budget, and imagining what it would take to sell pizza. After talking about how decimals, fractions, and percents all play a role in understanding quantity, I assigned students to groups.

One group looked at the label on a water bottle. The decimal measure indicated the amount was 1.25 pt. There was a second mixed number showing servings in the bottle: 2.5. Dealing with these two numbers together almost pushed the students to a new level of frustration. I refocused them by asking three questions. First I asked, "How do decimals help you?" The students answered, "They tell the size, the quantity." "How about fractions? How do they help you?" I continued. Without prompting, Raoul said, "They divide up the amount between two people." "What about percents then?" I wondered aloud. Maura turned the bottle to the nutrition facts and showed me 0%. When I asked the group to report back, the rest of the class gave them a round of applause for their clarity.

Martha Merson, Guest Teacher
Dimock Community Health Center, Roxbury, MA

Appendices

Name _____ Date _____

Using Benchmarks: Fractions, Decimals, and Percents

INITIAL ASSESSMENT

First check off how you feel about your ability to solve each task. Then complete the tasks that you can do.

Look at each task and decide whether you can do it, don't know how to do it, or are not sure if you can. Check off the appropriate choice, and then complete the task, if you can.

Task 1: Show and Tell What You Know about $\frac{1}{2}$

1. Show $\frac{1}{2}$ on each picture.

___ Can do   ___ Don't know how   ___ Not sure

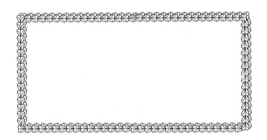 

2. What are other ways to write $\frac{1}{2}$?

___ Can do   ___ Don't know how   ___ Not sure

3. Other things I know about $\frac{1}{2}$:

___ Can do   ___ Don't know how   ___ Not sure

Task 2: Show and Tell What You Know about $\frac{1}{4}$

1. Show $\frac{1}{4}$ on each picture.

___ Can do   ___ Don't know how   ___ Not sure

2. What are other ways to write $\frac{1}{4}$?

___ Can do   ___ Don't know how   ___ Not sure

3. Other things I know about $\frac{1}{4}$:

___ Can do   ___ Don't know how   ___ Not sure

Task 3: Show and Tell What You Know about $\frac{3}{4}$

1. Show $\frac{3}{4}$ on each picture.

___ Can do   ___ Don't know how   ___ Not sure

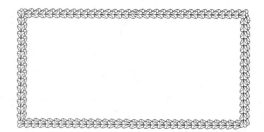   

2. What are other ways to write $\frac{3}{4}$?

___ Can do   ___ Don't know how   ___ Not sure

3. Other things I know about $\frac{3}{4}$:

___ Can do   ___ Don't know how   ___ Not sure

Task 4: Show and Tell What You Know about 0.1

1. What fraction does 0.1 represent?

___ Can do   ___ Don't know how   ___ Not sure

2. Other things I know about 0.1:

___ Can do   ___ Don't know how   ___ Not sure

Task 5: Find the Halfway Mark

Find and label the halfway mark on each of the following number lines:

1.

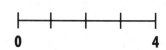

0   4

___ Can do   ___ Don't know how   ___ Not sure

2.

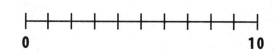

0   10

___ Can do   ___ Don't know how   ___ Not sure

3.

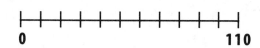

0   110

___ Can do   ___ Don't know how   ___ Not sure

4.

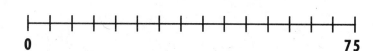

0   75

___ Can do   ___ Don't know how   ___ Not sure

Task 6: More Than, Less Than, or Equal To

1. $\frac{6}{10}$ is ___ more than $\frac{1}{2}$ ___ less than $\frac{1}{2}$ ___ equal to $\frac{1}{2}$
  ___ Can do   ___ Don't know how   ___ Not sure

2. $\frac{13}{27}$ is ___ more than $\frac{1}{2}$ ___ less than $\frac{1}{2}$ ___ equal to $\frac{1}{2}$
  ___ Can do   ___ Don't know how   ___ Not sure

3. $\frac{5}{21}$ is ___ more than $\frac{1}{4}$ ___ less than $\frac{1}{4}$ ___ equal to $\frac{1}{4}$
  ___ Can do   ___ Don't know how   ___ Not sure

4. $\frac{25}{60}$ is ___ more than $\frac{1}{4}$ ___ less than $\frac{1}{4}$ ___ equal to $\frac{1}{4}$
  ___ Can do   ___ Don't know how   ___ Not sure

5. $\frac{15}{50}$ is ___ more than $\frac{3}{4}$ ___ less than $\frac{3}{4}$ ___ equal to $\frac{3}{4}$
  ___ Can do   ___ Don't know how   ___ Not sure

6. $\frac{8}{12}$ is ___ more than $\frac{3}{4}$ ___ less than $\frac{3}{4}$ ___ equal to $\frac{3}{4}$
  ___ Can do   ___ Don't know how   ___ Not sure

Task 7: Water Bottles

Refer to the labels on the Cold Spring Water bottles to answer the questions.

1. Which bottle is the better deal? Explain how you know.

___ Can do   ___ Don't know how   ___ Not sure

2. Exactly how many ounces are in a full liter? Explain how you know.

___ Can do   ___ Don't know how   ___ Not sure

3. Exactly how many ounces are in a quarter liter? Explain how you know.

___ Can do   ___ Don't know how   ___ Not sure

INITIAL ASSESSMENT CLASS TALLY

Task		Can Do	Don't Know How	Not Sure	Percent Who Can Do
1.	1				
	2				
	3				
2.	1				
	2				
	3				
3.	1				
	2				
	3				
4.	1				
	2				
5.	1				
	2				
	3				
	4				
6.	1				
	2				
	3				
	4				
	5				
	6				
7.	1				
	2				
	3				

Notes on Confidence Levels

INITIAL ASSESSMENT CHECKLIST

Use a ✓, ✓+, or ✓– to assess how well students met each skill. When you give feedback to students, note areas in which they did well in addition to areas for improvement.

Use ✓ to show work that is mostly accurate; some details, additional work needed

Use ✓+ to show work that is accurate, complete.

Use ✓– to show work that is inaccurate, incomplete.

Student's Name_____

Task	Skills	Lesson Taught
1. Show 1/2 1 _____ 2 _____ 3 _____	Shows 1/2 with pictures Writes 1/2 in other forms Describes 1/2	1
2. Show 1/4 1 _____ 2 _____ 3 _____	Shows 1/4 with pictures Writes 1/4 in other forms Describes 1/4	2
3. Show 3/4 1 _____ 2 _____ 3 _____	Shows 3/4 with pictures Writes 3/4 in other forms Describes 3/4	3
4. Show 0.1 1 _____ 2 _____	Writes the fraction equivalent of 0.1 Describes 0.1	5, 6
5. Find the Halfway Mark 1 _____ 2 _____ 3 _____ 4 _____	Labels halfway mark on numberline segments	1

6. More Than, Less, Than, or Equal To		
1 _____	Compares fractions to 1/2	1
2 _____		
3 _____	Compares fractions to 1/4	2
4 _____		
5 _____	Compares fractions to 3/4	3
6 _____		
7. Water Bottles		
1 _____	Finds the better deal, comparing two bottles	
2 _____	Finds the whole, given the half	
3 _____	Finds one-fourth (ounces in a quarter liter)	

OVERALL NOTES

Strengths

_____

_____

_____

_____

_____

_____

_____

Areas for Improvement

_____

_____

_____

_____

_____

_____

_____

_____

EMPower™

Using Benchmarks: Fractions, Decimals, and Percents

FINAL ASSESSMENT

Look at each task and decide whether you can do it, don't know how to do it, or are not sure if you can. Check off the appropriate choice, and then complete the task if you can.

Task 1: Check out the Books

Refer to the bookshelves shown below to answer all the questions.

Bookshelf 1	Bookshelf 2	Bookshelf 3	Bookshelf 4	Bookshelf 5
Volcanoes	Fishing	Cooking	Mystery	Dinosaurs

1. For his science fair project, Daniel read $\frac{3}{4}$ of the books about volcanos that are on the shelf. How many books has he read?

___ Can do   ___ Don't know how   ___ Not sure

2. Ten percent of the fishing books on the shelf are about deep-sea fishing. What percent are not?

___ Can do   ___ Don't know how   ___ Not sure

Now write your answer using a fraction.

___ Can do   ___ Don't know how   ___ Not sure

3. The number of cookbooks on the shelf represents one-fourth of the total cook book collection. How many are missing?

___ Can do   ___ Don't know how   ___ Not sure

4. If Joseph took out $\frac{1}{2}$ of the mystery books on the shelf and Jill took out $\frac{3}{4}$ of the ones that were left, how many mystery books would remain?

___ Can do   ___ Don't know how   ___ Not sure

5. More than half of the dinosaur books on the shelf have illustrations by the same author. How many books could that be?

___ Can do   ___ Don't know how   ___ Not sure

Task 2: Marks and Labels

1. Miguel's mom hates that he turns the radio volume up so loud. What benchmark fraction best describes the volume setting?

___ Can do   ___ Don't know how   ___ Not sure

Volume

Low   High

2. Myra found a stain on her bandana 9/10 of the way from the top. Use an "X" to indicate where the stain might be.

___ Can do   ___ Don't know how   ___ Not sure

Top

Task 3: Population Statistics

1. Find the benchmarks for the number 6,000.

___ Can do ___ Don't know how ___ Not sure.

Benchmark Fraction	Percent Name	Decimal Name	The Fraction Based on 6,000 People	The Actual Number Based on 6,000 People
a. $\frac{1}{2}$				
b. $\frac{1}{4}$				
c. $\frac{3}{4}$				
d. $\frac{1}{10}$				

2. Due to high rates of HIV/AIDS in some parts of the world, in a village of 6,000 people, many people will be affected. Complete the statistics with actual numbers. Pay attention to the number for the whole group.

___ Can do ___ Don't know how ___ Not sure.

  a. The entire village, or ____% of the people, could be personally affected by HIV/AIDS.

  ___ Can do ___ Don't know how ___ Not sure.

  b. Twenty-three percent, or a little under _____ of children under 15, are orphans.

  ___ Can do ___ Don't know how ___ Not sure.

  c. If 3,000 of the village's population are children, what fraction of the village's population are children?

  ___ Can do ___ Don't know how ___ Not sure.

   (1) Between 0 and $\frac{1}{4}$

   (2) Between $\frac{1}{4}$ and $\frac{1}{2}$

   (3) Exactly half

   (4) Between $\frac{1}{2}$ and $\frac{3}{4}$

   (5) More than $\frac{3}{4}$

d. About one-tenth of the 3,000 children who are orphans are boys under three years old. The number of orphaned boys is about _____.

___ Can do   ___ Don't know how   ___ Not sure

e. The male orphans represent what part of the total population?

___ Can do   ___ Don't know how   ___ Not sure

(**1**) Between 0 and $\frac{1}{4}$

(**2**) Between $\frac{1}{4}$ and $\frac{1}{2}$

(**3**) Exactly half

(**4**) Between $\frac{1}{2}$ and $\frac{3}{4}$

(**5**) More than $\frac{3}{4}$

f. Between half and three-quarters of the 700 teenage girls are infected. The number of teenage girls who are infected could range from _____ to _____.

___ Can do   ___ Don't know how   ___ Not sure

g. Three out of every four families are caring for AIDS orphans. If there are about 1,000 households, _____ are caring for orphans.

___ Can do   ___ Don't know how   ___ Not sure

h. Three-quarters of the population, or _____, believe AIDS has many causes. They think the traditional way of men practicing unsafe sex with multiple partners is not a problem.

___ Can do   ___ Don't know how   ___ Not sure

i. Statisticians estimate that the number of orphans will reach 0.5 million in the entire country. This figure is

___ Can do   ___ Don't know how   ___ Not sure

(**1**) Between 0 and 250,000

(**2**) Between 250,000 and 500,000

(**3**) 500,000

(**4**) Between 500,000 and 750,000

(**5**) More than 750,000

Task 4: Body Weight

Casey, a six-month-old baby, weighs 20 pounds.

Complete the statements about Casey. Show your reasoning using words, pictures, or a number line.

1. If his body weight doubled in a year, he would weigh _____.

___ Can do   ___ Don't know how   ___ Not sure

2. If his body weight increased by 0.1 in one month, it would be _____.

___ Can do   ___ Don't know how   ___ Not sure

3. If his body weight increased by 50% in a year, he would weigh _____.

___ Can do   ___ Don't know how   ___ Not sure

4. If the neighbor's baby's weight was $\frac{1}{4}$ less than Casey's weight, she would weigh _____ pounds.

___ Can do   ___ Don't know how   ___ Not sure

5. Vera's weight would be what fraction of Casey's total weight? _____

___ Can do   ___ Don't know how   ___ Not sure

FINAL ASSESSMENT CHECKLIST

Use a ✓, ✓+, or ✓– to assess how well students met each skill. When you give feedback to students, note areas in which they did well in addition to areas for improvement.

Use ✓ to show work that is mostly accurate; some details, additional work needed.

Use ✓+ to show work that is accurate, complete.

Use ✓– to show work that is inaccurate, incomplete.

Student's Name_____

Task	Skills	Lesson Taught
1. Check out the Books		
1 _____	Finds 3/4 of an amount	3
2 _____	Finds the complement of 10%	6
3 _____	Finds an amount, given 1/4 of it	4
4 _____	Finds half of an amount and 3/4 of the remaining amount	3
5 _____	Gives an estimate for more than a half of an amount	1
2. Marks and Labels		
1 _____	Determines the fraction shown in a picture	3
2 _____	Locates a point 9/10 of the way	6
3. Volume		
1a _____	Finds benchmark fractions for 6,000	All
1b _____	Completes statements relying on benchmark fractions, decimals, and percents	All
1c _____		
1d _____		
2a _____		
2b _____		
2c _____		
2d _____		
2e _____		
2f _____		
2g _____		
2h _____		
2i _____		
4. Body Weight		
1 _____	Doubles 20	1
2 _____	Finds an increase of 0.1 of 20	6
3 _____	Determines 50% and adds it to given weight to find an increase	1
4 _____	Determines 1/4 less of an amount	2
5 _____	Compares part to whole as 3/4	3

OVERALL NOTES

Strengths

_____

_____

_____

_____

_____

_____

_____

Areas for Improvement

_____

_____

_____

_____

_____

_____

_____

0.1		
	$\dfrac{1}{10}$	1.0
$\dfrac{10}{1}$	10%	
$\dfrac{2}{10}$	.2	100%
	one-tenth	point one
1.1		10.0

Blackline Master 3: Mini Grids

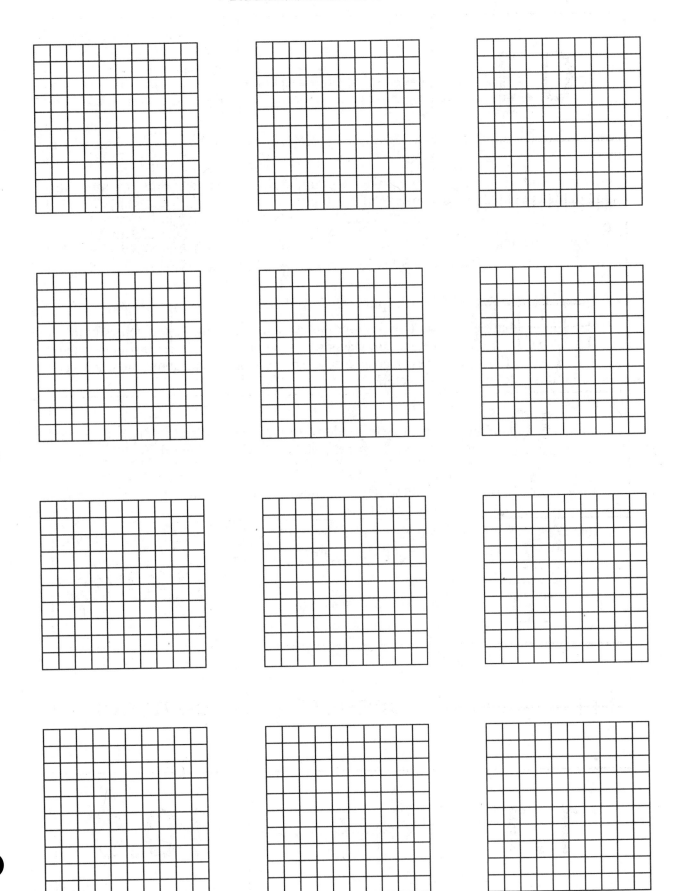

Decimals: "Let me tell you all right now, I am the easiest number to get along with because I am a lot like a whole number. I tell you exactly what I mean. If I say it is 12.2 ounces, it is. If I tell you it is 1.2 million, it is."

Percents: "Well, I think you just have low standards. If people are going to be tangling with me, they are going to do it on my terms."

Fractions: "And you can't do my job. Take, for example, this class. If you want to describe this class, you are nowhere with decimals. With fractions you can talk about 1/2 the class or 3/9 of the class. I have it all over you. Decimals, hah! What are you going to tell us?"

Decimals (coughing): "Well, if there were a part of something, I could tell you how much was in that part. Say you wanted to know how much water someone drank in a day. I could tell you that precisely."

Fractions: "Exactly my point. How helpful is that? And percents do not get the point right away."

Percents: "I would not even want to talk about this class. It is too tiny. Now if you want to relate to a class I have dealt with before, like any class of 100, then I could work with you. Fifty percent of the class, 25% of the class—we can go all over the board. We can talk about the whole class as 100%. But this piddling stuff—forget it."

Decimals: "Anyway, this class is just one example. Let's take some other examples."

Percents: "How about budgeting? How much do you pay for rent or taxes? What's the budget for starting a daycare center or park in your neighborhood? To talk about these things, you need percents."

Decimals: "Fine. How about buying something liquid—anything from gasoline to cough syrup to alcohol to milk. I'm best at describing these."

Fractions: "Perhaps, but once you use some of that liquid, you will need fractions to describe how much is left unless you use it all up at one time."

Blackline Master 6: 0.5 cm Grid Paper

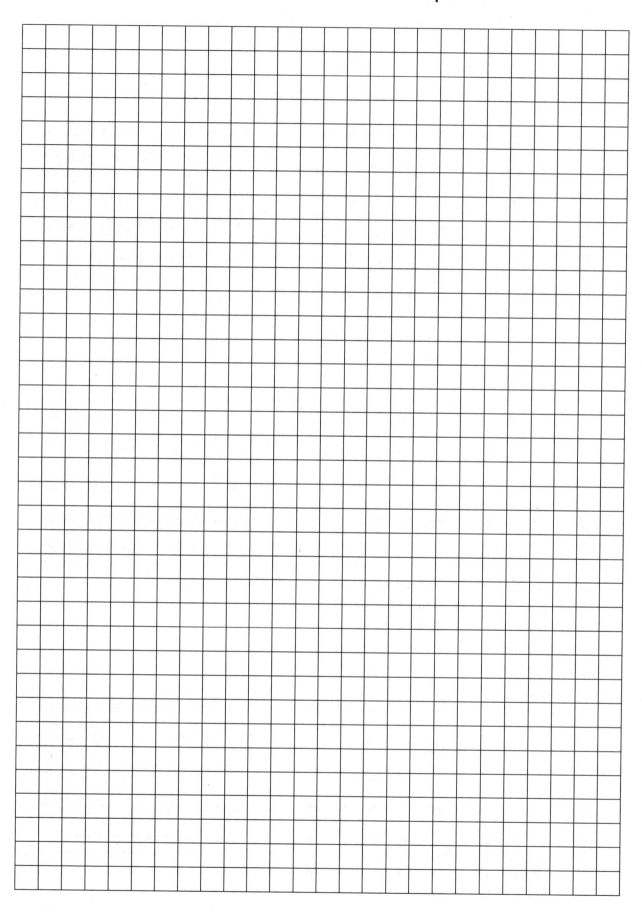

Blackline Master 7: Test Practice Answer Sheet

Test Practice

Name _____

Date _____

Lesson # _____

1. ① ② ③ ④ ⑤
2. ① ② ③ ④ ⑤
3. ① ② ③ ④ ⑤
4. ① ② ③ ④ ⑤
5. ① ② ③ ④ ⑤

6.
	/	·	0	1	2	3	4	5	6	7	8	9
	/	·	0	1	2	3	4	5	6	7	8	9
	/	·	0	1	2	3	4	5	6	7	8	9
	/	·	0	1	2	3	4	5	6	7	8	9
	/	·	0	1	2	3	4	5	6	7	8	9

Test Practice

Name _____

Date _____

Lesson # _____

1. ① ② ③ ④ ⑤
2. ① ② ③ ④ ⑤
3. ① ② ③ ④ ⑤
4. ① ② ③ ④ ⑤
5. ① ② ③ ④ ⑤

6.
	/	·	0	1	2	3	4	5	6	7	8	9
	/	·	0	1	2	3	4	5	6	7	8	9
	/	·	0	1	2	3	4	5	6	7	8	9
	/	·	0	1	2	3	4	5	6	7	8	9
	/	·	0	1	2	3	4	5	6	7	8	9

Test Practice

Name _____

Date _____

Lesson # _____

1. ① ② ③ ④ ⑤
2. ① ② ③ ④ ⑤
3. ① ② ③ ④ ⑤
4. ① ② ③ ④ ⑤
5. ① ② ③ ④ ⑤

6.
	/	·	0	1	2	3	4	5	6	7	8	9
	/	·	0	1	2	3	4	5	6	7	8	9
	/	·	0	1	2	3	4	5	6	7	8	9
	/	·	0	1	2	3	4	5	6	7	8	9
	/	·	0	1	2	3	4	5	6	7	8	9

Glossary

Reminder: Students generate their own definitions for terms as they arise in class, using language that makes sense to them. However, to help you guide the discussion, we include mathematical definitions for most of the terms.

Italicized terms are *not* included in the *Student Book,* but are included in the *Teacher Book* as background information. The lesson number in which the term first appears is in parentheses following the term.

benchmark (1)—a familiar number used as a point of reference. For example, 1/2 is a benchmark fraction because it can be used easily as a point of reference for comparing quantities greater than or less than a half.

decimal (Opening)—in this book, the term used to label a number with one or more digits to the right of the decimal point. For example, 5.1 and 0.54 are decimal numbers. More generally, "decimal" refers to any number in the base-10 system .

***decimal point* (6)**—a symbol used to separate dollars from cents in money and the ones place from the tenths place in decimal numbers.

fraction (Opening)—a number that indicates a certain part of one whole or a part of a group of things. For example,

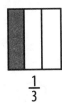

$\frac{1}{3}$

$\frac{1}{3}$

***gauge* (6)**—a standard or scale of measurement or an instrument for measuring. For example, the gasoline gauge in a car indicates how much gasoline there is in the tank. A gauge on a thermometer is given either in degrees Fahrenheit or degrees Centigrade.

one-half, half (Opening)—one of two equal parts of a whole. For example, if half of the cars in a parking lot are red, the other half—an equal number—are not red.

one-quarter, one-fourth, 1/4 (2)—one out of four parts of a whole. For example, if one-fourth of the people in a group of 40 are not Democrats, it means that 10 are not Democrats and the other 30 are. In money, one-quarter is $0.25. In this book, one-fourth is also called "a half of a half."

one-tenth (5)—a decimal or fraction that names one part of 10 equal parts. For example, a dime is one-tenth of a dollar because a dime has 10 cents and a dollar has 100 cents.

part (1)—a portion related to the whole. For example, in 3/4, "3" is the part and "4" is the whole.

***pattern*—a set of shapes, numbers, or actions that are repeated in a predictable way. Patterns may be described by a rule using numbers, words, or mathematical symbols such as *x, y,* and *z.*

percent (Opening)—the ratio of a number to 100; percent means "per hundred." For example, 25% is 25 out of 100.

***rounding*—a type of estimation or approximation that makes it easier to work with numbers. For example, if you are counting clips and there are 148, you might round to 150, the nearest 10. With fractions, if you are considering 3/7, you might round to 1/2 because 3/7 is close to 1/2, and 1/2 is a much "friendlier" fraction to use.

statistic (Closing)—numerical information about a group, for example, "Over 12% of the population of the United States in 2003 were age 65 and over."

***Tithe* (5)**—any voluntary contribution that consists of one-tenth of someone's income.

three-fourths, three-quarters (3)—the remaining portion of a whole after 1/4 is considered. For example, if Sam eats 1/4 of the cookies, then 3/4 of the cookies are left over. In time, 3/4 of an hour is 45 minutes because an hour has four 15-minute groups.

whole (1)—the entire object, collection of objects, or quantity being considered, 100%.

Answer Key

Opening the Unit

Activity 1: Making a Mind Map
Answers will vary.

Activity 2: I Will Show You 1/2! Part 1
Answers will vary. See *Opening the Unit* for sample responses.

Activity 2: I Will Show You 1/2! Part 2

1. a.

   1 day
   | 24 hours | 12 hours | 12/24 | 1/2 |

   2 days
   | 48 hours | 24 hours | 24/48 | 1/2 |

   5 days
   | 120 hours | 60 hours | 60/120 | 1/2 |

   10 days
   | 240 hours | 120 hours | 120/240 | 1/2 |

   b. The part numbers are half of the whole numbers.

2.
   $1
   | 100 pennies | 50 pennies | 50/100 | 1/2 |

   $2
   | 200 pennies | 100 pennies | 100/200 | 1/2 |

   $5
   | 500 pennies | 250 pennies | 250/500 | 1/2 |

   $10
   | 1000 pennies | 500 pennies | 500/1000 | 1/2 |

3. Answers will vary. Sample answer: Divide the number by 2 to find 1/2 of it.

Activity 3: Initial Assessment
Refer to the *Initial Assessment Checklist*, p. 93, and *Looking Closely*, p. 8, for suggestions when observing students.

Task 1: Show and Tell What You Know about 1/2
1. Answers will vary, but each picture should represent 1/2.
2. Answers will vary. Anticipated answers include one-half, 50%, and one out of two.
3. Answers will vary.

Task 2: Show and Tell What You Know about 1/4
1. Answers will vary, but each picture should represent 1/4.
2. Answers will vary. Anticipated answers include one-fourth, 25%, and one out of four.
3. Answers will vary.

Task 3: Show and Tell What You Know about 3/4
1. Answers will vary, but each picture should represent 3/4.
2. Answers will vary. Anticipated answers include three-fourths, 75%, and three out of four.
3. Answers will vary.

Task 4: Show and Tell What You Know about 0.1
1. One-tenth
2. Answers will vary.

Task 5: Find the Halfway Mark
1. Halfway mark at 2
2. Halfway mark at 5
3. Halfway mark at 55
4. Halfway mark at 37.5

Task 6: More Than, Less Than, or Equal to

1. More than 1/2
2. Less than 1/2
3. Less than 1/2
4. Less than 1/2
5. Less than 1/2
6. More than 1/2

Task 7: Water Bottles

1. One is not better than another. The bottle with 16.9 oz. is the same as the 0.5 liter bottle and costs half the price of a full liter.
2. About 34 ounces (33.8). Answers will vary. Students may realize that there are 355 mL in 12 fl. oz. From there, they may be able to figure out that there are 33.8 oz. in 1000 mL, or 1 L.
3. About 8.5 ounces (8.45). Answers will vary.

Lesson 1: Sharing Secret Designs

Activity 1: Stations – Comparing Fractions to 1/2

Item at Each Station	Part	Whole	Fraction	Equal to, Greater than, Less than 1/2
Station 1	16 days	30 days	16/30	greater than

Answers will vary for Stations 2–5, depending on materials used.

Activity 2: Is It Half?

1.

Fraction for the Total	Fraction Described in the Story	Fraction for Half
80/80	60/80	40/80

a. More than 1/2 the whole box.

2.

Fraction for the Total	Fraction Described in the Story	Fraction for Half
15/15	7/15	7.5/15

b. Less than 50% of his money.

3.

Fraction for the Total	Fraction Described in the Story	Fraction for Half
500/500	228/500	250/500

b. Less than 50% of the ream.

4.

Fraction for the Total	Fraction Described in the Story	Fraction for Half
7/7	3.5/7	3.5/7

c. Halfway to work.

5.

Fraction for the Total	Fraction Described in the Story	Fraction for Half
4/4	3/4	2/4

a. More than 1/2 a muffin.

6.

Fraction for the Total	Fraction Described in the Story	Fraction for Half
3/3	1.5/3	1.5/3

c. 1/2 the flour she needs.

Practice: Half the Size

1.

2.

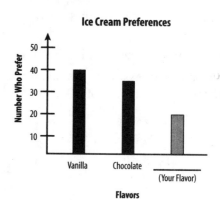

3.

a.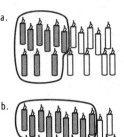

b.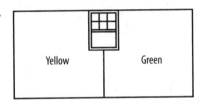

4. a.

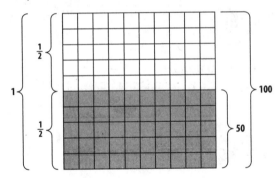

Yellow   Green

    b. Answers will vary.

    c. Answers will vary.

5. a. Halfway between Mt. Ramo and the diner. It looks to be halfway around the circle.

    b. 125 miles; 125 is half of 250.

Practice: Why Is 50% a Half?

Answers will vary. A sample answer using the grid may look like this:

$\frac{1}{2}$ {
1 {
$\frac{1}{2}$ {

} 100

} 50

Practice: Find Half of It

1. 2 million
2. 375,000 people
3. 44-year-old
4. 8-oz. chocolate bar
5. 12.5-percent increase
6. 15-day billing cycle
7. 45° angle
8. 200 years of oppression
9. 1/2 mile of swimming, or 36 laps
10. 27 days until summer vacation

Practice: Choose an Amount

1. Answers will vary but should be more than 8 but less than 16 oz.
2. Answers will vary but should be more than 15 but less than 30 days.
3. Answers will vary but should be more than 0 but less than 45°.
4. Answers will vary but should be more than 44 but less than 88 years.
5. Answers will vary but should be more than 2 million but less than 4 million.
6. Answers will vary but should be more than 375,000 but less than 750,000.
7. Answers will vary but should be more than 0 but less than 1 1/2 cups.
8. Answers will vary. Sample answer: I would divide the total amount by 2.
9. Answers will vary. Sample answer: I would add half the amount twice to find the total amount.

Practice: More "Is It 1/2?" Problems

1. a
2. b
3. b

Methods for figuring out the answers will vary.

Practice: What Is the Whole?

1.

1/2 the Number	The Whole Number	Fraction for the Whole
15	30	30/30
75	150	150/150
3 1/2	7	7/7
335	670	670/670
22.5	45	45/45

2. $320
3. 1,500 calories
4. 39 pounds
5. 18 are not immigrants; 36 people altogether

Practice: Which Is Larger?

1. 5/8; 2/5 is less than 1/2, but 5/8 is more than 1/2 (4/8 = 1/2).
2. 3/4; 1/3 is less than 1/2, but 3/4 is more than 1/2 (2/4 = 1/2).

3. They are equal; 8/16 is the same as 1/2, and 6/12 is the same as 1/2.

4. 4/7; 4/9 is less than 1/2, but 4/7 is more than 1/2 (3.5/7 = 1/2).

Extension: Half a Million?

1. 1,000,000

2. a

3. b

4. c

5. Possible answers: Crystal and Santa Linda (for a total of 700,000) or Jackson and Santa Linda (for a total of 850,000). Explanations will vary.

6. Answers will vary.

Test Practice

1. (3)

2. (3)

3. (2)

4. (2)

5. (5)

6. 50%

Lesson 2: Half of a Half

Activity 1: 1/4 Wasted

1. **a.** 1/4 wasted = 5 pounds
   3/4 left = 15 pounds

   b. 1/4 wasted = 20.5 pounds
   3/4 left = 61.5 pounds

   c. 1/4 wasted = 500 pounds
   3/4 left = 1,500 pounds

2. **a.** 1/4 wasted = $2.50
   3/4 left = $7.50

   b. 1/4 wasted = $1.25
   3/4 left = $3.75

   c. 1/4 wasted = $22.50
   3/4 left = $67.50

3. **a.** Total available work time is 4 hours.

   b. Total available work time is 10 hours.

   c. Total available work time is 26 hours.

   d. Total available work time is 192 hours.

4. **a.** 96 books to start

   b. 480 books to start

   c. 228 books to start

5. **a.** 25% = 30 hired; 75% = 90 not hired

   b. 36 actors in all

   c. 100 called in all; 75 hired to work on the set

Activity 2: Is It Really a Quarter?

Answers will vary.

Practice: What Makes It a Quarter?

Answers will vary. For example, 25¢ out of the 100¢ are shaded, and that is one-fourth; or three portions just like the one that is shaded are *not* shaded, making four altogether, with one shaded.

Practice: Show Me 1/4!

1.

   a. The total number of pieces is 4.

   b. The number of shaded pieces is 1.

   c. The fraction is 1/4.

2.

   a. The total number of pieces is 8.

   b. The number of shaded pieces is 2.

   c. The fraction is 2/8, or 1/4.

3.

   a. The total number of pieces is 12.

   b. The number of shaded pieces is 3.

   c. The fraction is 3/12, or 1/4.

4.

   a. The total number of units in the number line is 4.

   b. The number of shaded units is 1.

   c. The fraction is 1/4.

5.

1.5

a. The total number of units in the number line is 6.

b. The number of shaded units is 1.5.

c. The fraction is 1.5/6, or 1/4.

6.

a. The total number of units in the number line is 16.

b. The number of shaded units is 4.

c. The fraction is 4/16, or 1/4.

Practice: 1/4 Measurements

1.

2.

3.

4. 1/4 of 12 is 3; the mark should be on the 3.

5. 1/4 of 16 is 4; the mark should be on the 4.

6. 1/4 of 5 pounds = 1.25 pounds

7. 1/4 of 10 kilograms = 2.25 kilograms

8. 1/4 of a day = 6 hours

9.

1/4 of 60 minutes = 15 minutes

10. Answers will vary.

Practice: How Many, How Far?

1. a. 60 candies because 45 + 15 = 60

   b. Lucia got 15/60, or 1/4 (15 = part, 60 = whole).

   c. Yes. Answers will vary.

   d. Answers will vary.

   b. Answers will vary.

2. a. Between the 4th and 5th block

   b. At the 9th block

   c. Answers will vary.

3. a. 1/4; 2 eggs is 1/4 of 8 eggs

   b.

Super Gooey Brownies	Brownies with Only 2 Eggs
1 c. (cup) butter	1/4 c. (cup) butter
8 eggs	2 eggs
3 c. sugar	3/4 c. sugar
2 c. flour	1/2 c. flour
2 tsp. vanilla	1/2 tsp. vanilla
6 oz. unsweetened chocolate	1 1/2 oz. unsweetened chocolate

   c. Answers will vary.

   d. Answers will vary.

4. Three out of 10 is more than 1/4.

5. a. Shana contributes $3 an hour to health-care benefits.

   b. With a raise, Shana would pay less than 1/4 of her new wages to health-care benefits.

6. Legislators want to cut $50 million of the budget.

Practice: Comparing Fractions to 1/4

1. a. 8 days of rain out of 30
      8 days
      30 days
      8/30
      Greater than 1/4

   b. 125 yards run in the 440-yd. dash
      125 yards
      440 yards
      125/440
      Greater than 1/4

   c. 20 minutes out of an hour-long test
      20 minutes
      60 minutes
      20/60
      Greater than 1/4

d. 1,320 feet walked out of a mile
1,320 feet
5,280 feet
1320/5280
Equal to 1/4

2. Answers will vary.

Extension: Which Is Larger?

1. a. 4/9; 4/9 is almost 1/2, but 2/8 is only 1/4.

   b. 5/8; 5/8 is more than 1/2, but 3/10 is less than 1/2.

   c. 3/12; 3/12 is cut into 12 equal parts, which is the same as 1/4; 3/16 is cut into 16 equal parts, so 3/16 is less than 1/4.

   d. 3/8; 1/3 is 3 out of 9 parts or 3/9, which is less than 3/8.

Test Practice

1. (2)

2. (5)

3. (1)

4. (5)

5. (2)

6. 75

Lesson 3: Three Out of Four

Activity 1: Seats for 3/4

1. Building A: 36;
   Building B: 75;
   Building C: 180

2. Building A: 48/48;
   Building B: 100/100;
   Building C: 240/240

3. Building A: 36/48;
   Building B: 75/100;
   Building C: 180/240

4. Building A: 12/48;
   Building B: 25/100;
   Building C: 60/240

5. Answers will vary.

6. Answers will vary.

7. Answers will vary.

Activity 2: Where Are You From?

1. Answers will vary. Sample answer: 8/32, or 1/4, of the people were from the United States.

2. a. (1) Less than 3/4 of the group.

   b. Answers will vary.

3. a. (3) 3/4 of the group.

   b. Answers will vary.

Practice: Show Me 3/4!

1.

   a. The total number of pieces is 4.

   b. The number of shaded pieces is 3.

   c. The fraction is 3/4.

2.

   a. The total number of pieces is 8.

   b. The number of shaded pieces is 6.

   c. The fraction is 6/8, or 3/4.

3.

   a. The total number of pieces is 12.

   b. The number of shaded pieces is 9.

   c. The fraction is 9/12, or 3/4.

4.

   a. The total number of units in the number line is 4.

   b. The number of shaded units is 3.

   c. The fraction is 3/4.

5.

   a. The total number of units in the number line is 6.

   b. The number of shaded units is 4.5.

   c. The fraction is 3/4.

6.

    a. The total number of units in the number line is 16.

    b. The number of shaded units is 12.

    c. The fraction is 3/4.

Practice: 3/4 Measurements

1.

2.

3.

4. 3/4 of 12 is 9; the mark should be on the 9.

5. 3/4 of 16 is 12; the mark should be on the 12.

6. 3/4 of 6 pounds = 4.5 pounds

7. 3/4 of 12 kilograms = 9 kilograms

8. 3/4 of a day = 18 hours

9.

3/4 of 60 minutes = 45 minutes

10. Answers will vary.

Practice: Where to Place It?

1.

4/14 < 3/4

2.

15/20 = 3/4

3.

2/3 < 3/4

4.

45/60 = 3/4

5. Answers will vary.

Practice: More "How Many, How Far?" Problems

1. a. 5 miles out of 24 is less than 1/4 because 6/24 = 1/4.

    b.

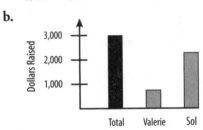

2. a. They stopped at the 15th block.

    b. 7 minutes

Practice: Missing Quantities – Parts and Wholes

1–6.

	$\frac{1}{4}$	$\frac{3}{4}$	$\frac{4}{4}$
1.	12 = 12 | 12 | 12 | 12	12 | 12 | 12 | 12 So $\frac{3}{4}$ is 36	If 12 people is $\frac{1}{4}$, and $\frac{4}{4}$ is 4 × 12, then 48 is the whole, or $\frac{4}{4}$.
2.	4 = $\frac{1}{4}$ 4 | 4 | 4 | 4	12 = $\frac{3}{4}$ 4 | 4 | 4 | 4	16 = $\frac{4}{4}$ 4 | 4 | 4 | 4
3.	3 = $\frac{1}{4}$ 3 | 3 | 3 | 3	9 = $\frac{3}{4}$ 3 | 3 | 3 | 3	12 = $\frac{4}{4}$ 3 | 3 | 3 | 3
4.	10 = $\frac{1}{4}$ 10 | 10 | 10 | 10	30 = $\frac{3}{4}$ 10 | 10 | 10 | 10	40 = $\frac{4}{4}$ 10 | 10 | 10 | 10
5.	6 = $\frac{1}{4}$ 6 | 6 | 6 | 6	18 = $\frac{3}{4}$ 6 | 6 | 6 | 6	24 = $\frac{4}{4}$ 6 | 6 | 6 | 6
6.	15 = $\frac{1}{4}$ 15 | 15 | 15 | 15	45 = $\frac{3}{4}$ 15 | 15 | 15 | 15	60 = $\frac{4}{4}$ 15 | 15 | 15 | 15

7. Answers will vary.

Extension: 3/4 of a Million?

1. **b.** Less than 3/4 of a million
2. **a.** More than 3/4 of a million
3. **a.** More than 3/4 of the number sold in Washington

Test Practice

1. (3)
2. (3)
3. (2)
4. (4)
5. (5)
6. $125

Lesson 4: Fraction Stations

Activity: Fraction Stations

See *Looking Closely* for suggestions on what to look for as students describe their data in fractional terms.

Practice: Less Than, More Than, Equal to, or Between?

1. More than 3/4
2. Equal to 3/4
3. Between 1/2 and 3/4
4. More than 3/4
5. Between 1/2 and 3/4
6. Between 1/4 and 1/2
7. Answers will vary.

Extension: Describing Data

1. **a.** (1) Less than 1/4 of the household's total
   b. (4) More than 3/4 of the household's total
   c. (3) Between 1/2 and 3/4 of the household's total
2. **a.** (5) Exactly 50% of the total
   b. (1) Less than 25% of the total
3. **a.** (2) Between 25% and 50% of the total
   b. (1) Less than 25% of the total

Extension: Fractions of Billions

1. 72/100 (or 18/25)
2. 72/100 is just under 3/4 (which is the same as 75%)
3. 17/100
4. Answers will vary. 17/100 is less than 1/4 (or 25%)

Test Practice

1. (2)
2. (2)
3. (4)
4. (3)
5. (1)
6. 1/2

Lesson 5: One-Tenth

Activity 1: Show Me 1/10 Stations

See *Looking Closely* for suggestions on what to look for as students describe their data in fractional terms.

Activity 2: Ways to Represent 1/10

Answers will vary.

Practice: I Will Show You 1/10!

1. One dime represents one-tenth.
2. 1 year
3. 2 pages
4. 4 beads
5. 450 voters

Practice: Containers

1.

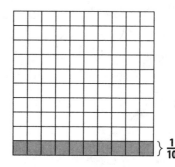

2.

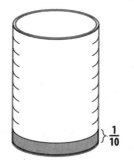

3.

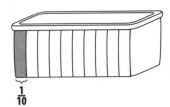

$\frac{1}{10}$

4.

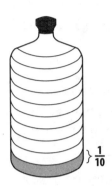

$\}\frac{1}{10}$

Practice: More or Less?

1. More than one-tenth (3/20 is more than 2/20, or 1/10.)

2. More than one-tenth (4/40 is more than 1/10.)

3. Less than one-tenth (23/230 is the same as 1/10, but she has read only 12/230.)

4. More than one-tenth (1/2 mile is the same as 5/10, which is more than 1/10.)

Extension: More Tenths

1. $180. One-tenth is $60, so 5/10, or 1/2, is $300. She has saved $120 already, so she needs $180 more.

2. 600 cups. One-quarter of a 10-hour day is 2 1/2 hours. 240 cups in 1 hour × 2 1/2 hours = 600.

Test Practice

1. (1)

2. (3)

3. (3)

4. (2)

5. (4)

6. $1,450

Lesson 6: More About One-Tenth

Activity 1: One-Tenth Match

See *Looking Closely* for suggestions on what to look for as students determine what fraction their cards represent.

Activity 2: One-Tenth, Nine-Tenths

1. Answers will vary.

2. Answers will vary.

3. Answers will vary.

4. Answers will vary.

Activity 3: Why Is 10% Equal to 1/10?

Answers will vary.

Practice: Make a Gauge

Answers will vary. Sample gauge:

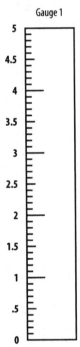

Gauge 1

5
4.5
4
3.5
3
2.5
2
1.5
1
.5
0

Practice: Location, Location, Location

1.

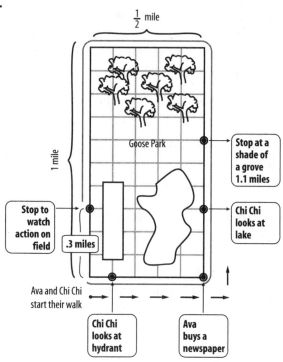

2. See graph above.
3. See graph above.
4. See graph above. They have walked 1.1 miles.
5. See graph above.
6. They need to walk 0.3 miles to get back to their starting point.

Practice: Gaining Weight

1.

Claudia	155	15.5 lb.	170.5 lb.	139.5 lb.
Salvatore	200	20 lb.	220 lb.	180 lb.
Jackie	110	11 lb.	121 lb.	99 lb.
Sue	180	18 lb.	198 lb.	162 lb.
Calvin	250	25 lb.	275 lb.	225 lb.
Lamika	135	135 lb.	148.5 lb	1215 lb.
Igor	140	14 lb.	154 lb.	125 lb.

2. See chart above.

Practice: Grid Visions

Part 1

1.

2.

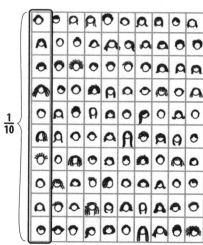

3.

Reprinted with permission of *World Education*

Part 2

1. 0.1 of 30 = 3
2. 0.1 of 50 = 5
3. 0.1 of 120 = 12
4. Answers will vary.
5. Answers will vary.
6. Answers will vary.

Extension: Reimbursement Changes

1. Answers will vary. Sample answer: You could figure out how much 1/10 of $130 is and then add it to $130 to see if it's the same as $143.
2. Answers will vary. Sample answer: You could figure out how much 1/10 of $110 is and then add it to $110 to see if it's the same as $121.
3. Answers will vary. Sample answer: You could figure out how much 1/4 of $20 is and then add it to $20 to see if it's the same as $25.
4. Answers will vary. Sample answer: You could figure out how much 1/10 of $20 is and then add it to $20 to see if it's the same as $22.

EMPower™

5.

Job	Adult Care Change from 2003	Childcare Change from 2003
Speech Therapist	+1.25	+0.6
Psychologist	+0.1	+0.57
Social Worker	+0.03	+0.1
Nursing Assistant	+0.25	+0.1
Occupational Therapist	–0.17	+0.32

Test Practice

1. (2)
2. (1)
3. (4)
4. (3)
5. (2)
6. 26

Closing the Unit

Activity 1: Standing Up

Answers will vary.

Activity 2: Review Session

Answers will vary.

Activity 3: Final Assessment

Refer to the *Final Assessment Checklist*, p. 100, and *Looking Closely*, p. 82, for suggestions when observing students.

Task 1: Check Out the Books

1. 6 books
2. 90% or 9/10
3. 12 books are missing.
4. 2 books
5. Answers will vary but should be at least 4 books.

Task 2: Marks and Labels

1. 3/4
2.

Stain should appear in the shaded region of the bandana.

Task 3: Population Statistics

1. **a.** 1/2   50%   0.5   3,000/6,000
      3,000

   b. 1/4   25%   0.25   1,500/6,000
      1,500

   c. 3/4   75%   0.75   4,500/6,000
      4,500

   d. 1/10   10%   0.10   600/6,000
      600

2. **a.** 100
   b. 1,500
   c. (3) Exactly 1/2
   d. 300
   e. (1) Between 0 and 1/4
   f. 350 to 525
   g. 750
   h. 4,500
   i. (3) 500,000

Task 4: Body Weight

1. 40 pounds
2. 22 pounds
3. 30 pounds
4. 15 pounds
5. 3/4

Sources and Resources

Mathematics Education

The National Council of Teachers of Mathematics (NCTM) publishes several excellent resources.

- *Principles and Standards for School Mathematics.* Reston, VA: NCTM, 2000.

- The NCTM journals: *Mathematics Teaching in the Middle Grades, Mathematics Teacher,* and *Journal for Research in Mathematics Education.*

- *Developing Number Sense in the Middle Grades, The Addenda Series, Grades 5–8.* Reston, VA: NCTM, 1991.

- *Historical Topics for the Mathematics Classroom.* Reston, VA: NCTM, 1989.

- http://www.nctm.org.

Fendel, D., D. Resek, L. Alper, & S. Fraser. *Interactive Mathematics Program.* Berkeley, CA: Key Curriculum Press, 1997.

Lappan, G., J. Fey, W. Fitzgerald, S. Friel, & E. Phillips. *Connected Mathematics Series.* Parsippany, NJ: Dale Seymour Publications, Division of Pearson Education, 1998.

Mokros, J., S.J. Russell, and K. Economopoulos. *Beyond Arithmetic: Changing Mathematics in the Elementary Classroom.* Palo Alto, CA: Dale Seymour Publications, 1995.

Morrison, P., and P. Morrison. *Powers of Ten.* New York: Scientific American Library, 1994.

National Research Council. *Adding It Up: Helping Children Learn Mathematics.* J. Kilpatrick, J. Swafford, and B. Findell (Eds.). Mathematics Learning Study Committee, Center for Education, Division of Behavioral and Social Sciences and Education. Washington, DC: National Academy Press, 2001.

Rasmussen, S. and D. *Key to Fractions.* Berkeley, CA: Key Curriculum Press, 1988.

Russell, S.J., et al. *The Investigations in Number, Data, and Space Curriculum.* White Plains, NY: Dale Seymour Publications, 1998.

Mathematics and Numeracy Education for Adults

Curry, D., M.J. Schmitt, and S. Waldron. *A Framework for Adult Numeracy Standards: The Mathematical Skills and Abilities Adults Need to Be Equipped for the Future.* Boston: World Education, 1996. (This framework was developed by members of the Adult Numeracy Network.) http://shell04.the world.com/std/anpn.

Massachusetts Department of Education. *Massachusetts Adult Basic Education Curriculum Frameworks for Mathematics and Numeracy.* Malden, MA: Massachusetts Department of Education, 2001. http://www.doe.mass.edu/acls/frameworks.

Stein, S. *Equipped for the Future Content Standards: What Adults Need to Know and Be Able to Do in the Twenty-First Century.* ED Pubs document EX0099P. Washington, DC: National Institute for Literacy, 2000.

Web Sites

http://www.funbrain.com/fract/

http://www.kidsolr.com/math/fractions.html

http://www.mcwdn.org/FRACTIONS/Equivalents.html

http://math.rice.edu/~lanius/Patterns/

http://www.coolmath4kids.com/fractions